Marcus and the enchanted farm

An adventure on Marcus's farm

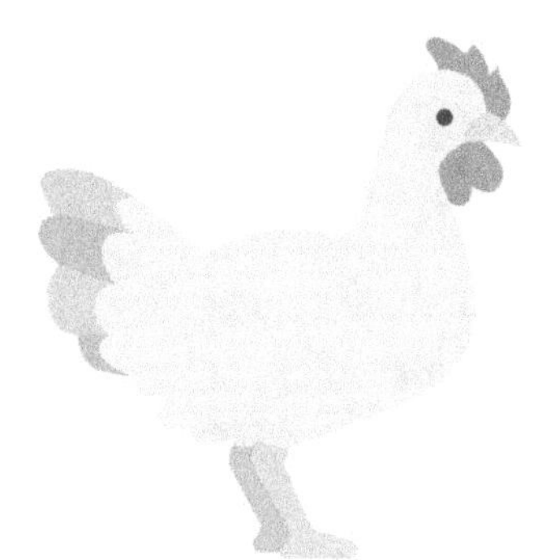

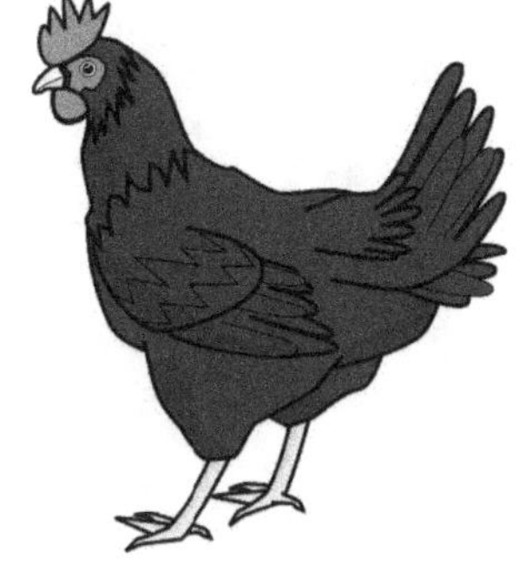

Idelmar dos santos   2024

HELLO

Bem-vindos a fazenda do Marcus! Preparem-se para embarcar em uma aventura extraordinária, cheia de surpresas e maravilhas. Nesta fazenda, você encontrara animais de várias espécies, plantas de vários tipos e segredos escondidos em cada canto. A imaginação é o seu guia, então desvende cada mistério que os espera nesta fazenda.Juntem-se a nós nesta jornada emocionante e descubram a beleza que os aguarda. Divirtam-se, queridos leitores.

ready? let's start

I am grateful to God for everything, and I believe that the meaning of life is to give meaning to other lives

I.S.P*

Idelmar dos Santos publicaions

test color page

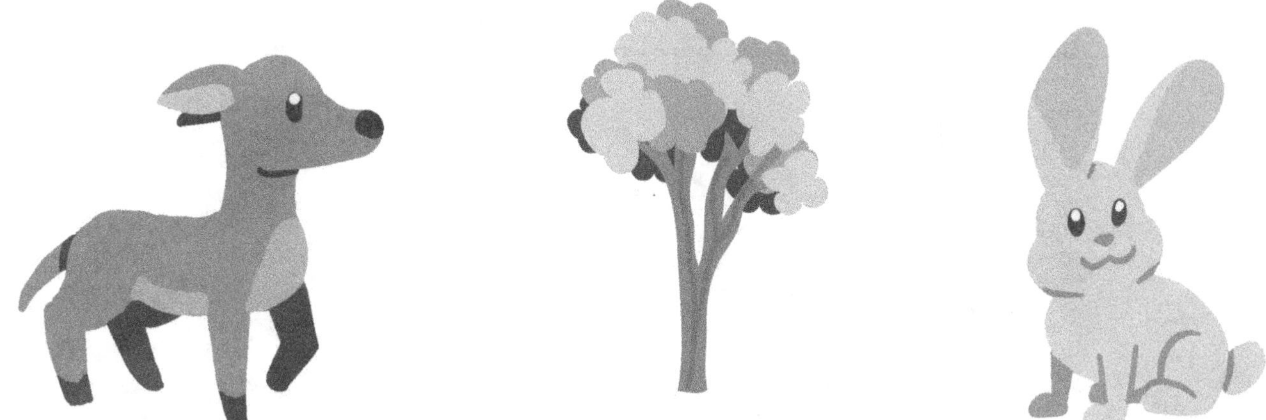

This book belongs to

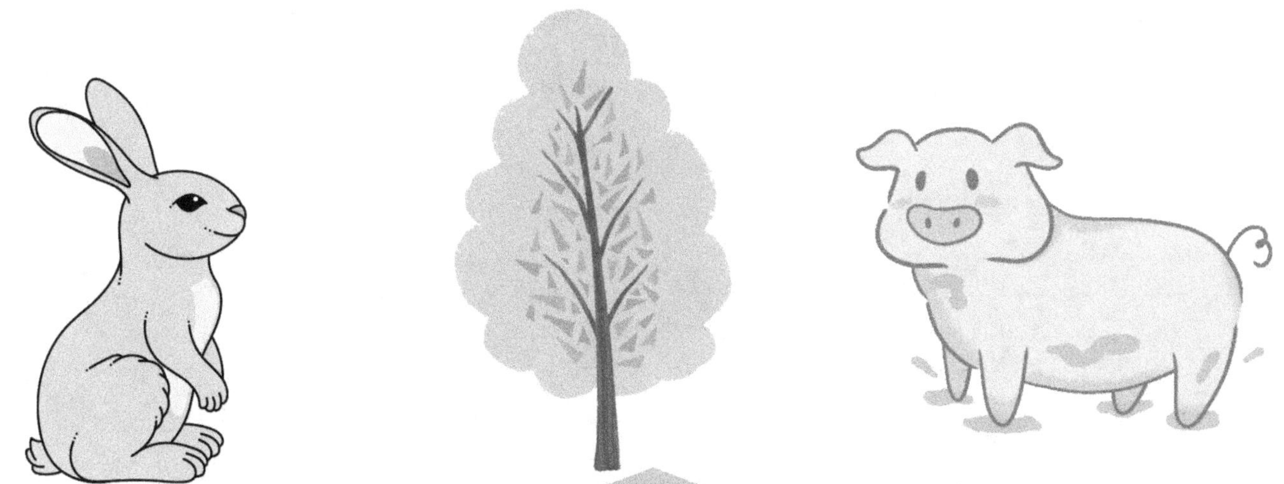

four to thirteen

Marcus lives and takes care of his farm with love.

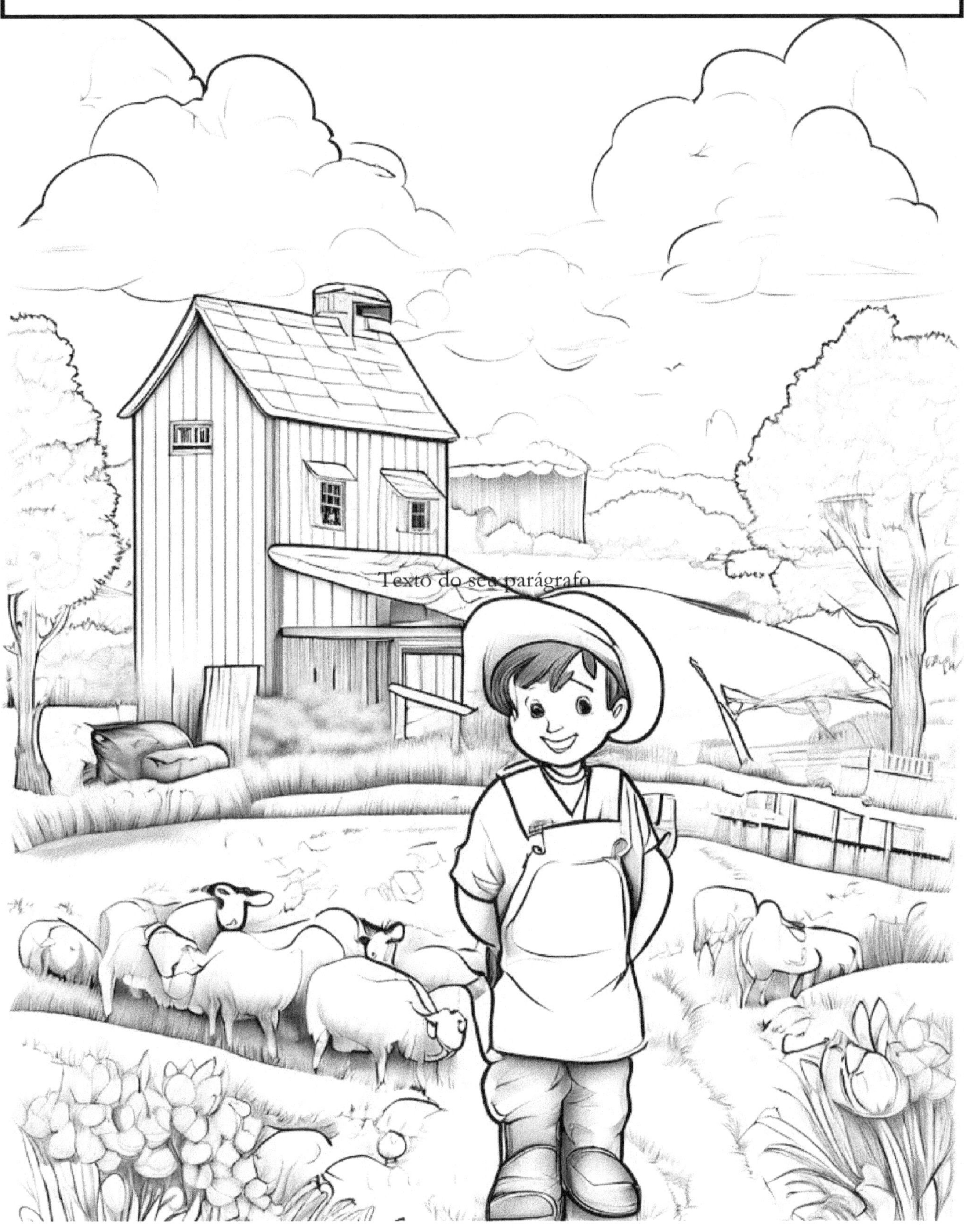

Marcus loved taking care of his garden, with vegetables.

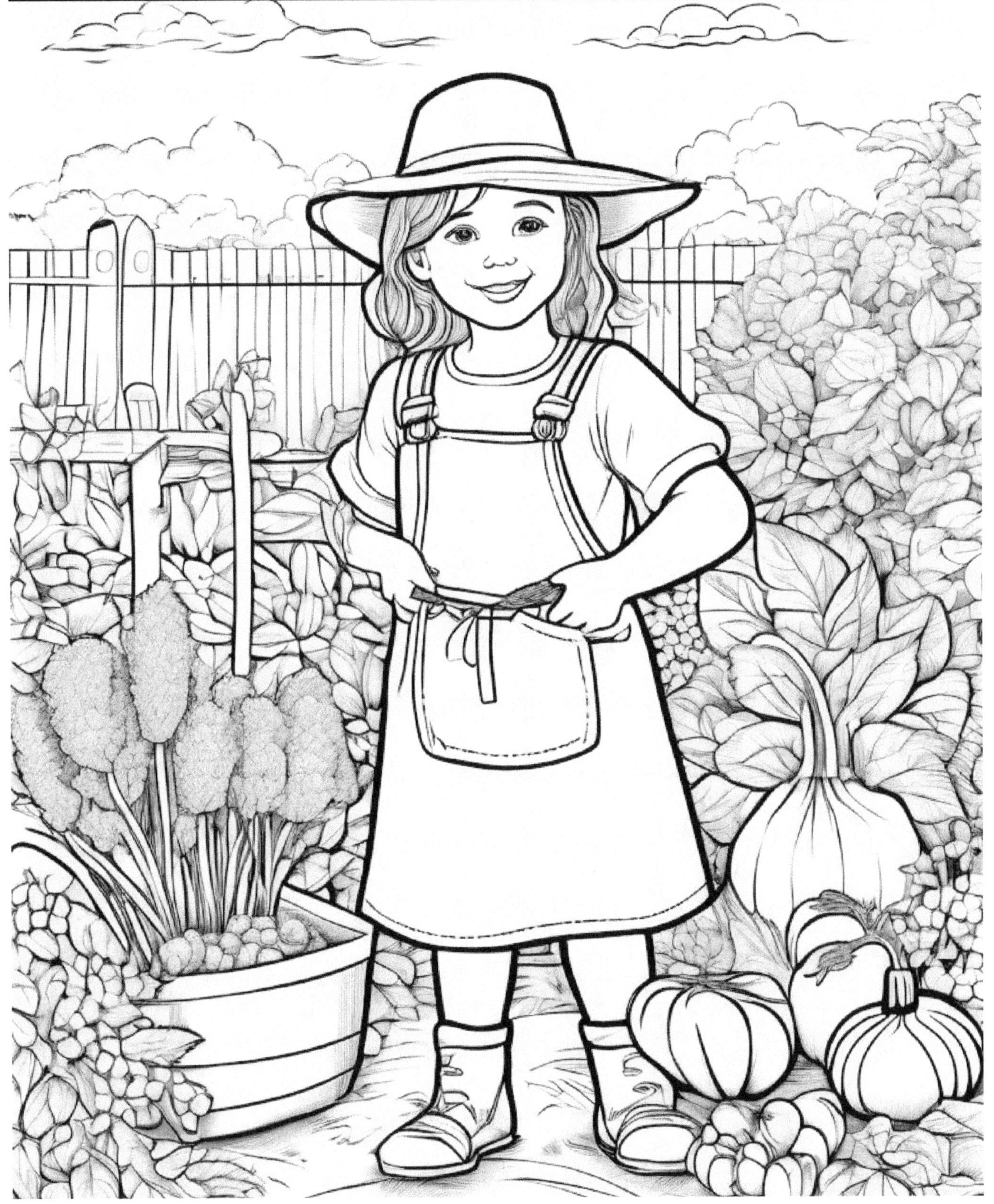

vegetables.

Marcus also had a horse called Lightning.

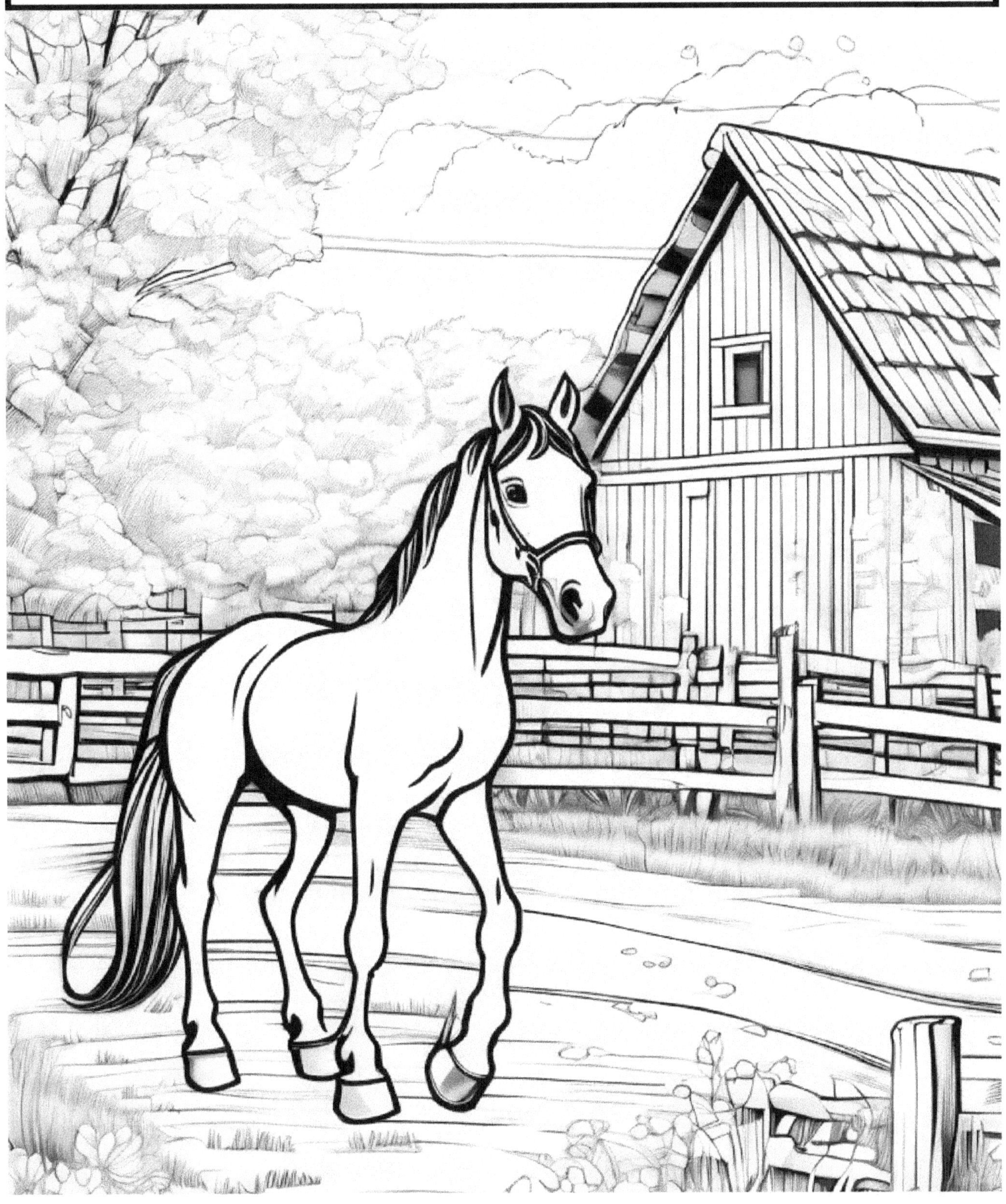

Marcus rode his horse and rode through the fields.

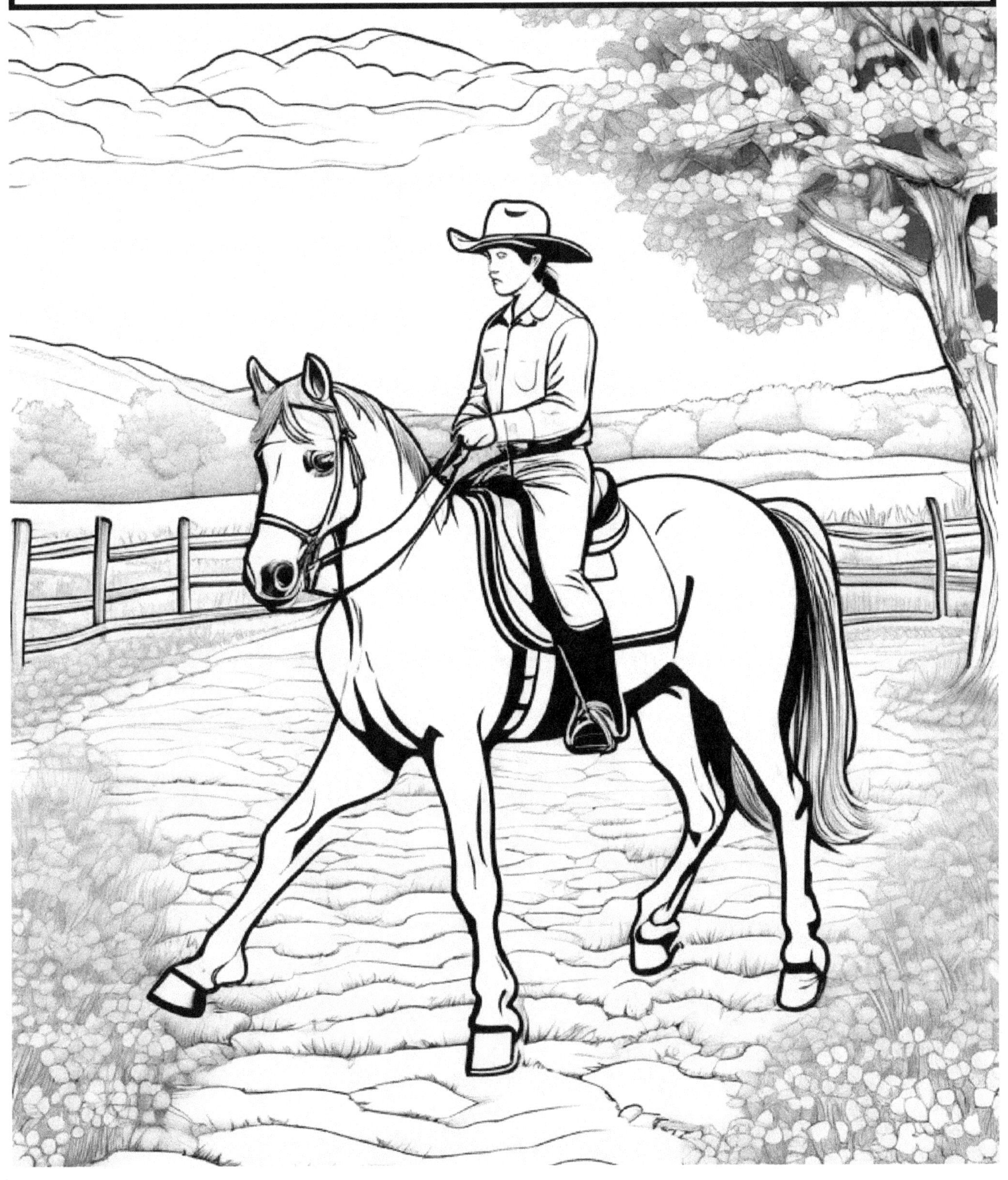

On Marcus's farm, there were several pigs in pigsties.

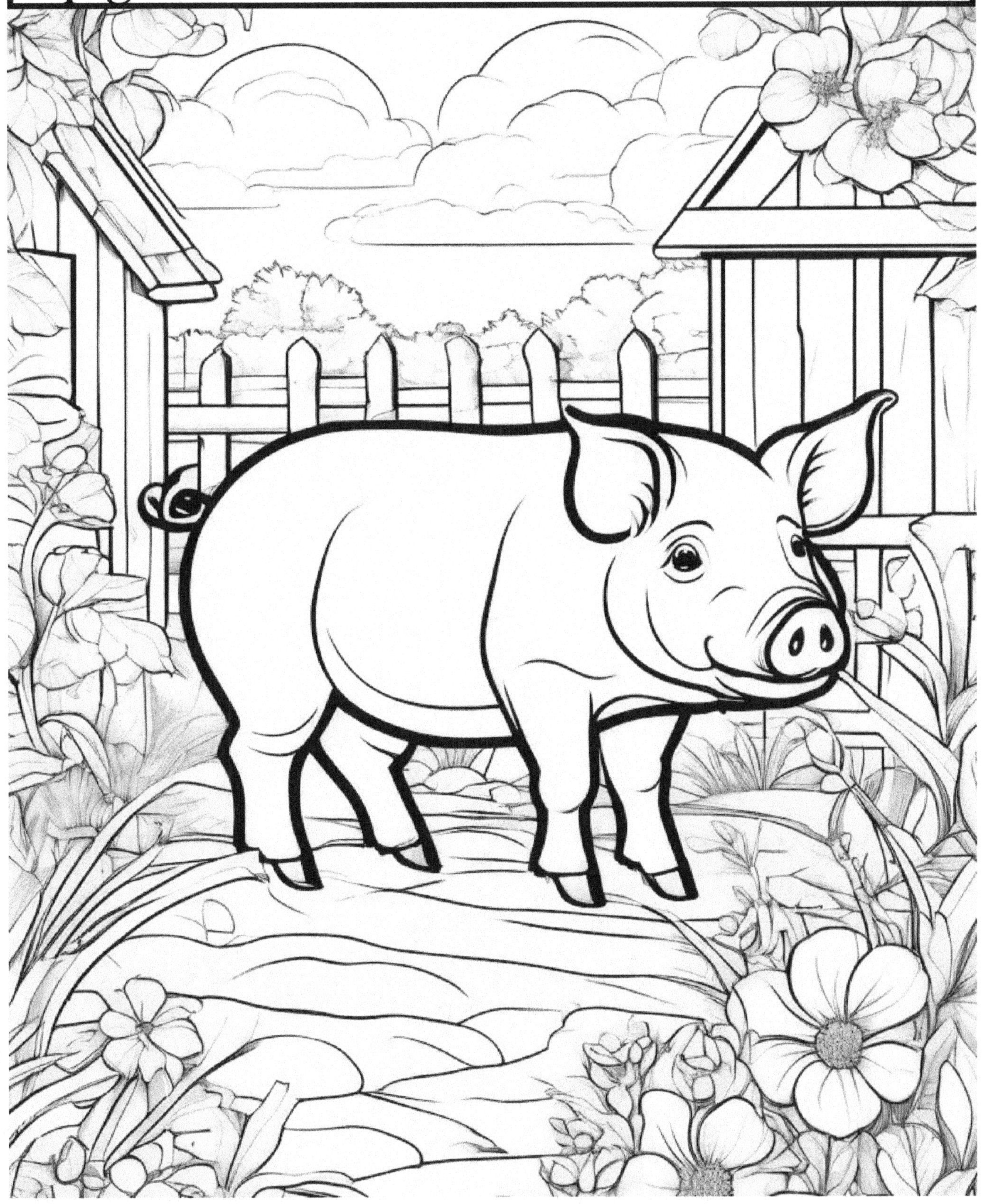

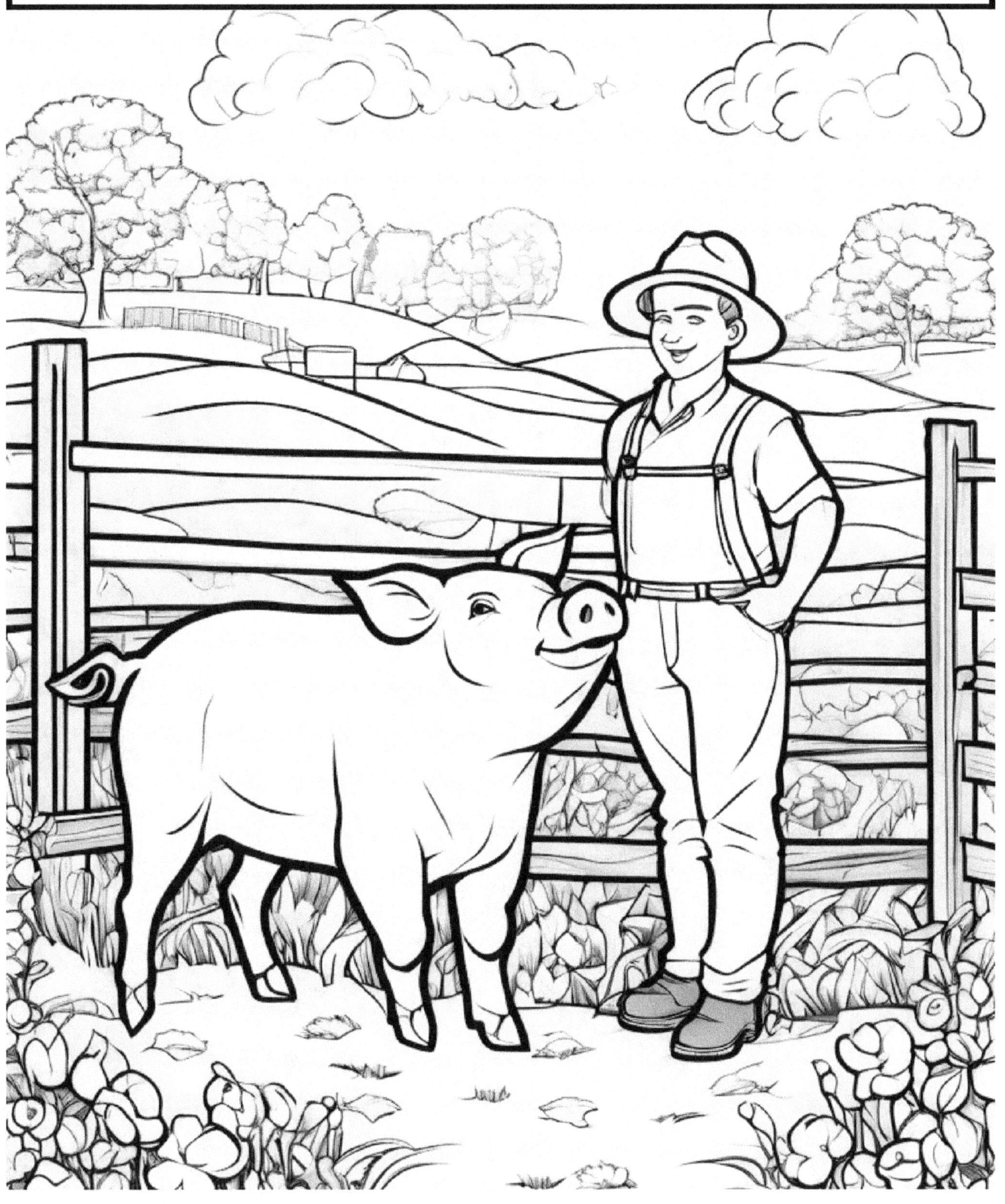

Marcus fed the pigs and had fun watching them.

In the middle of the garden, there was a loyal dog named Bob

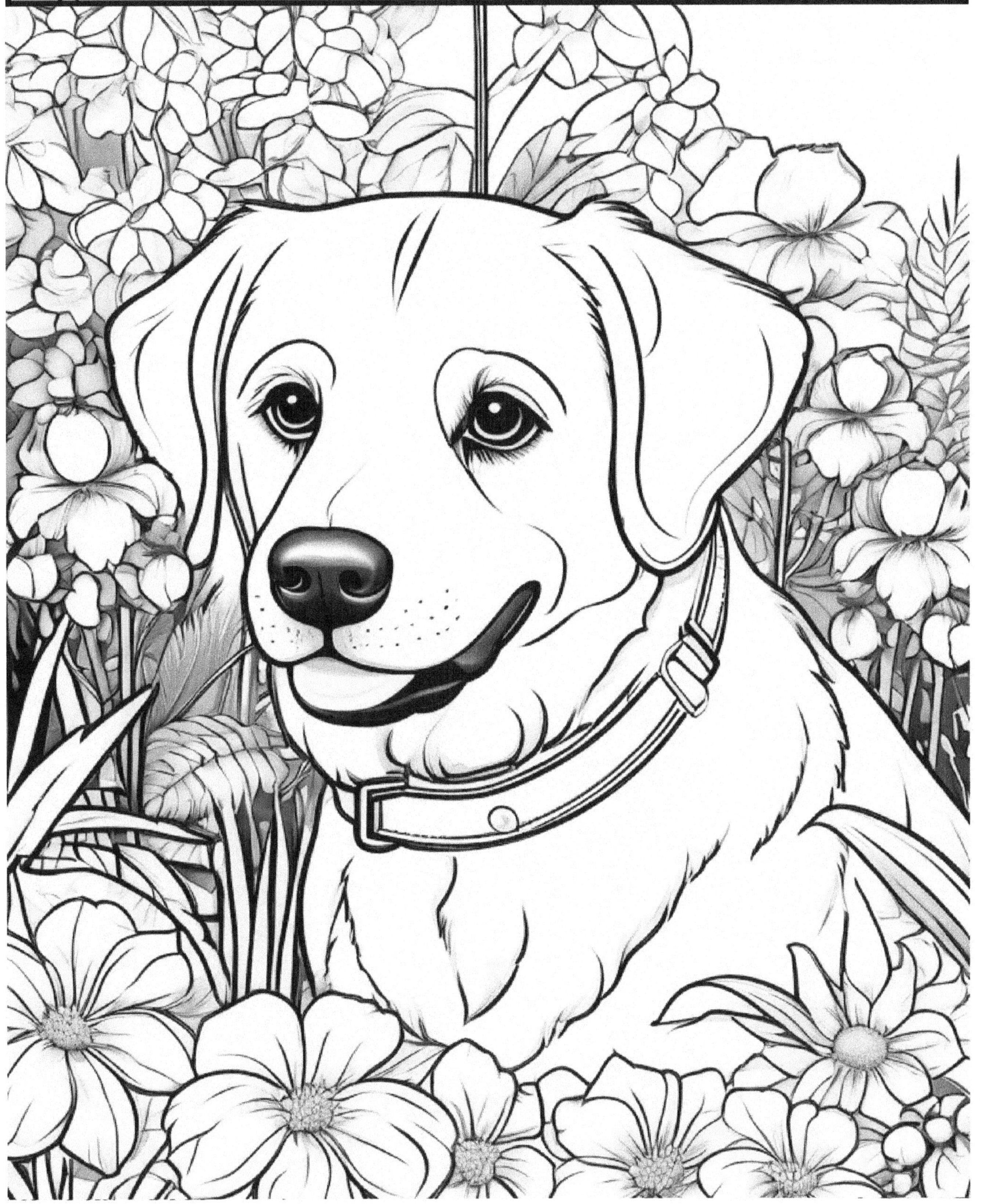

In the middle of the garden, there was a loyal dog named Bob

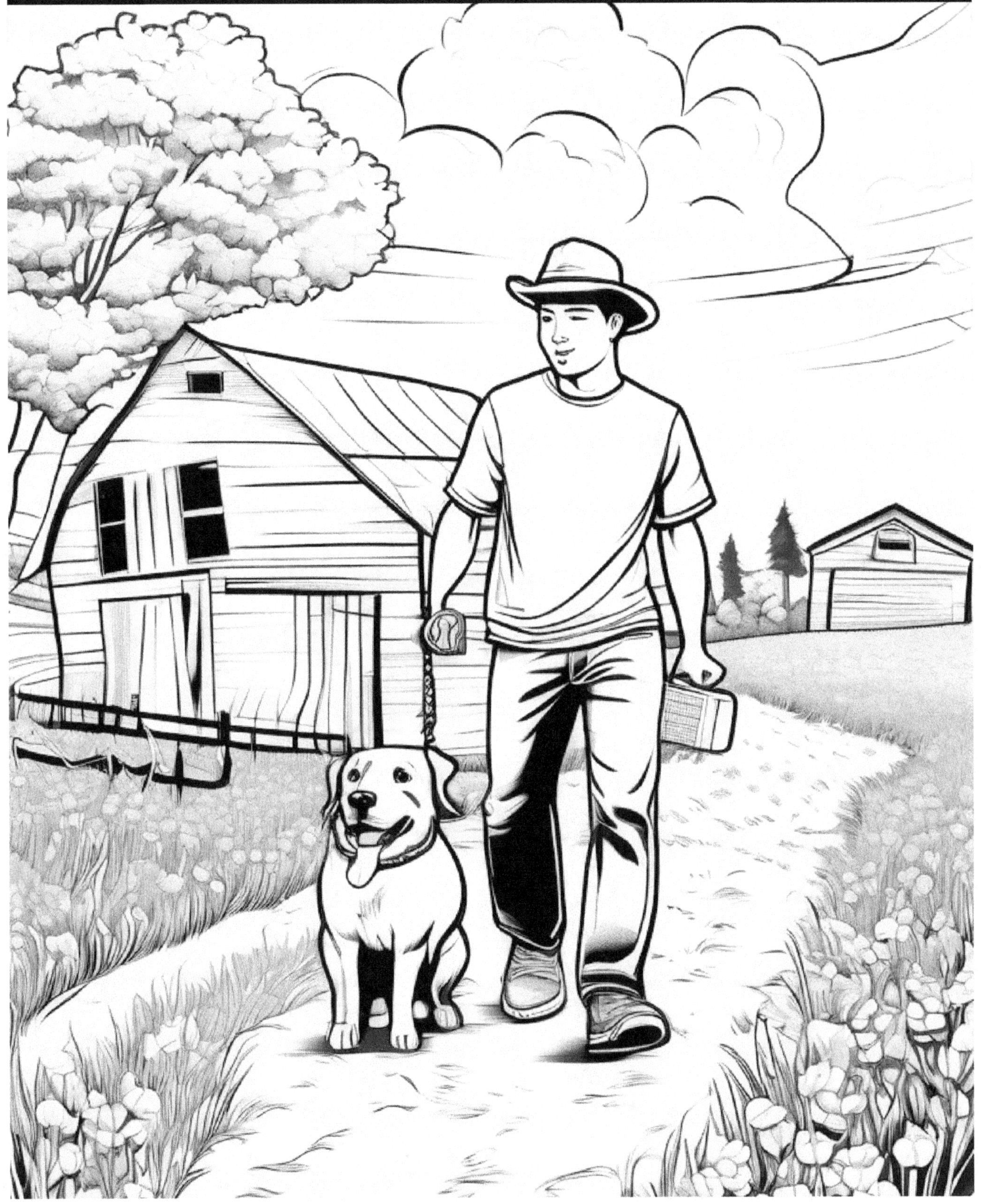

Bob protected the farm and was Marcus's best friend.

Bob loved chasing balls and playing.

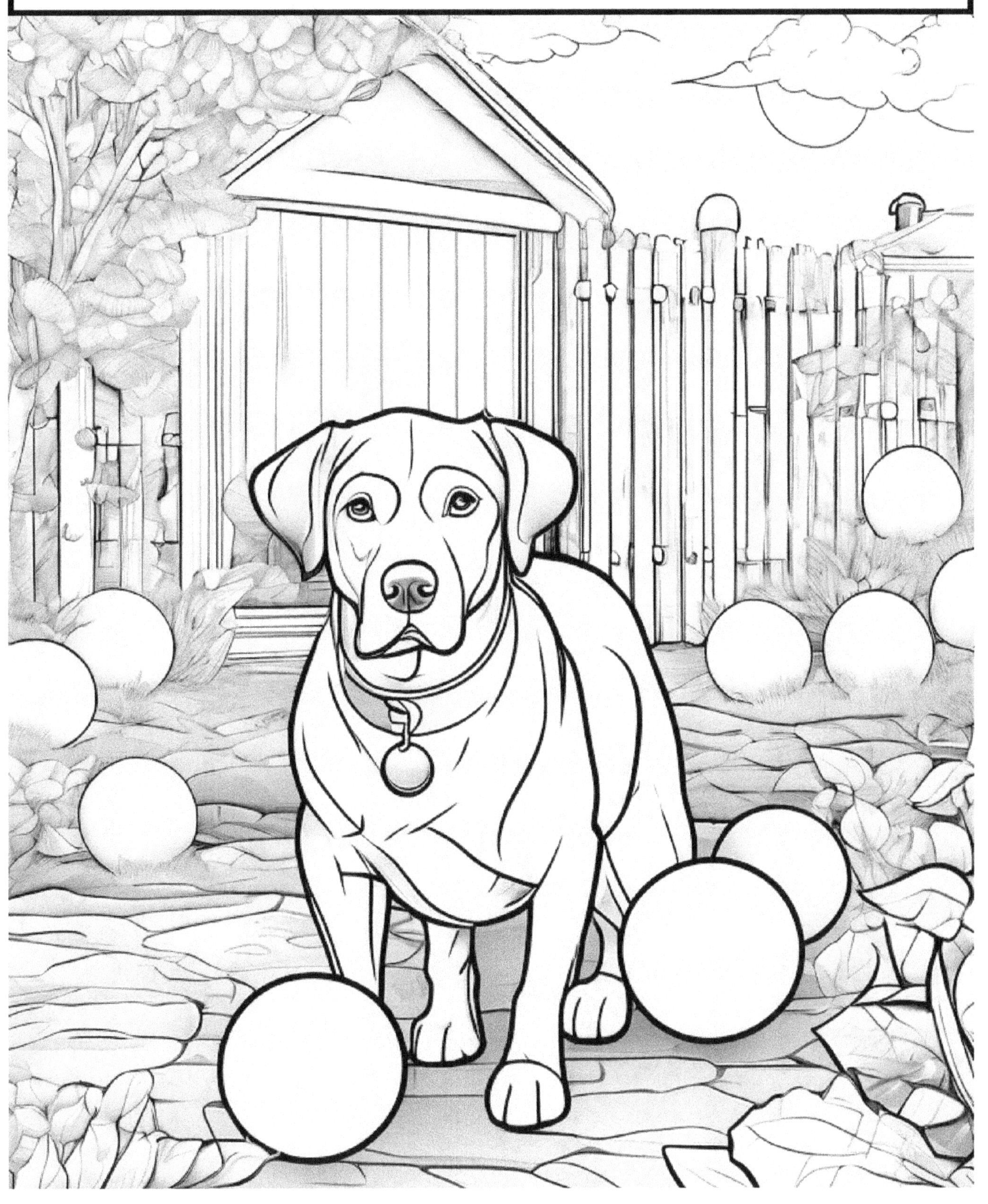

With the children who visited the farm.

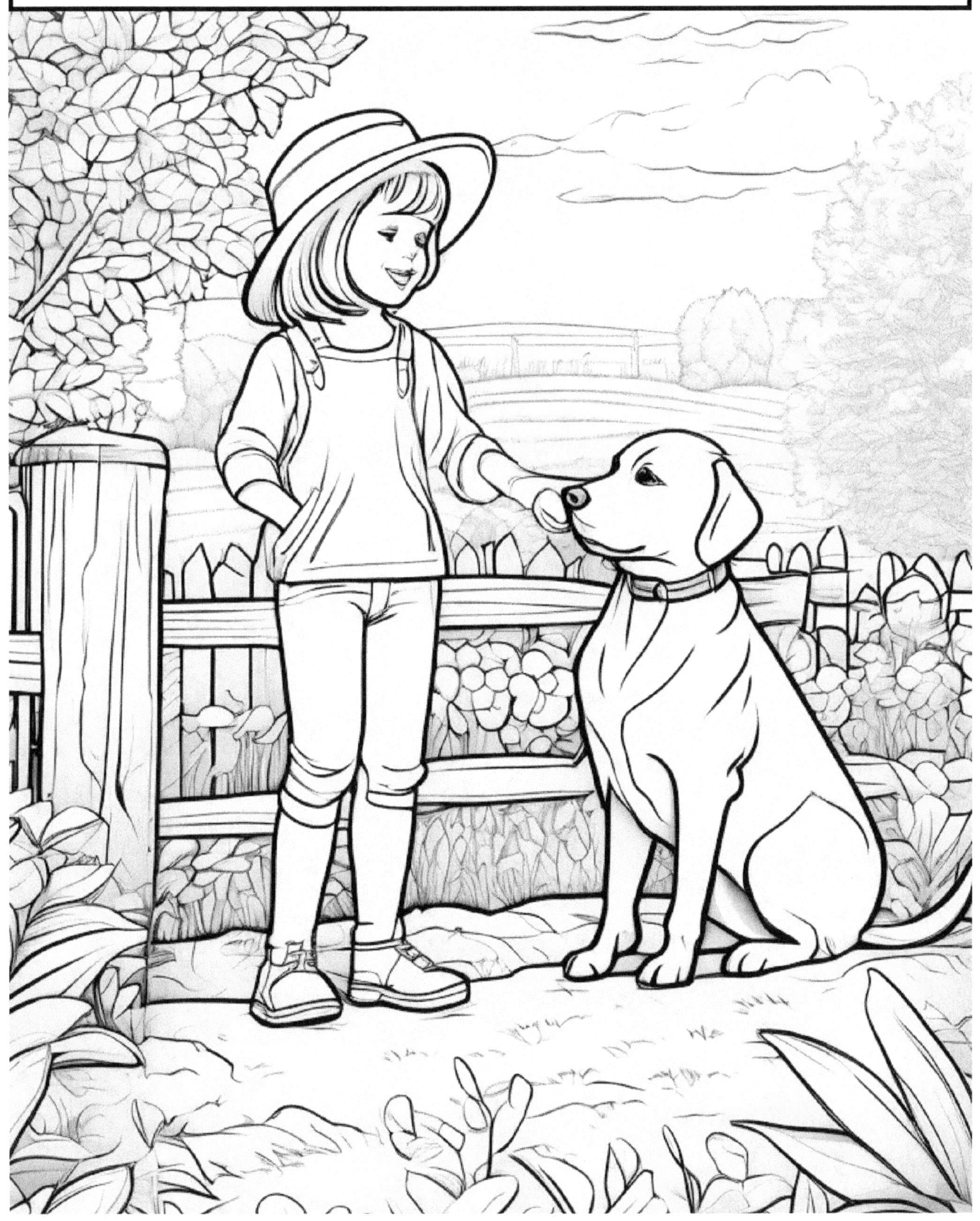

There are huge chickens in the farm's chicken coop.

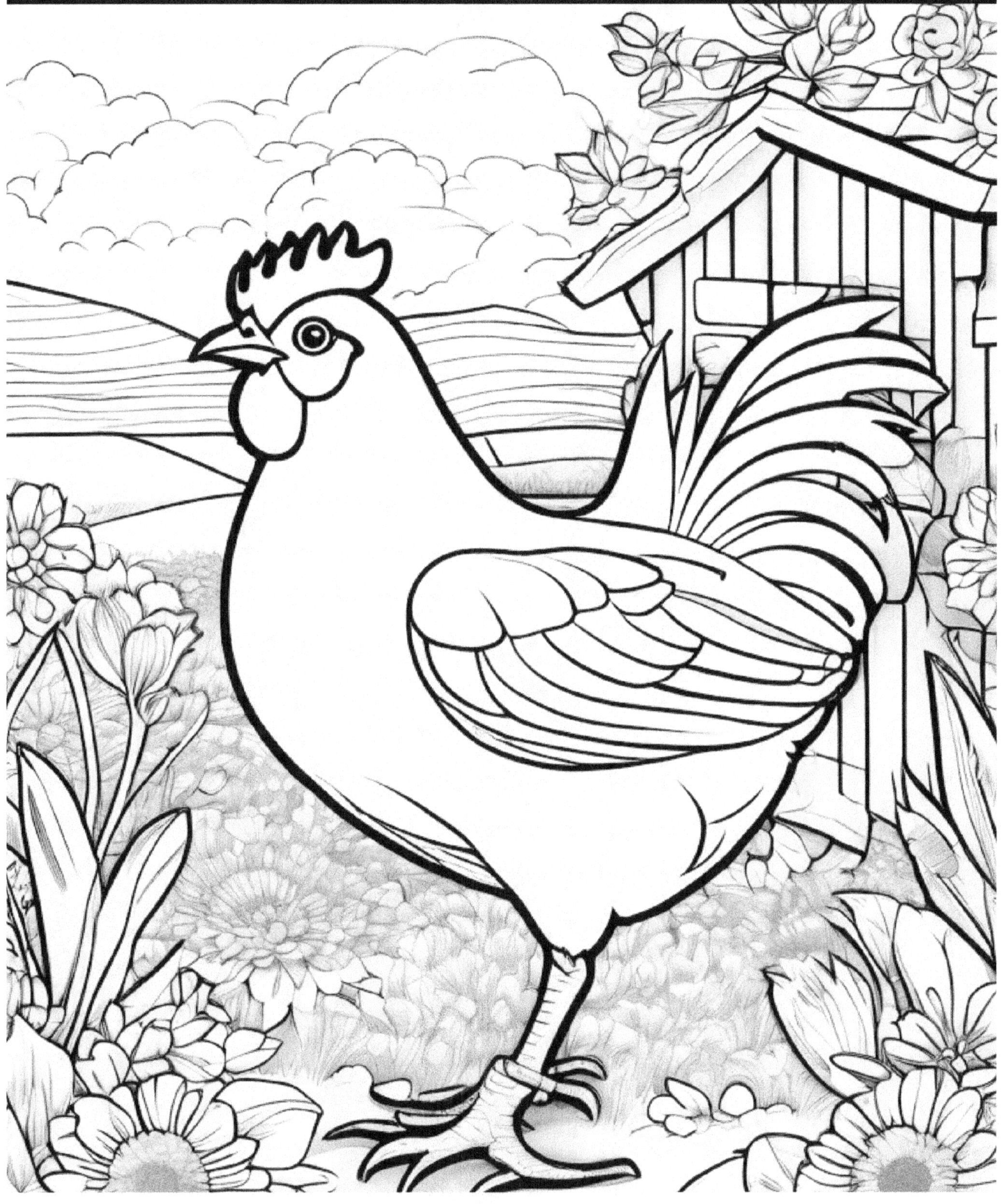

Who scratched the ground in search of worms and grain.

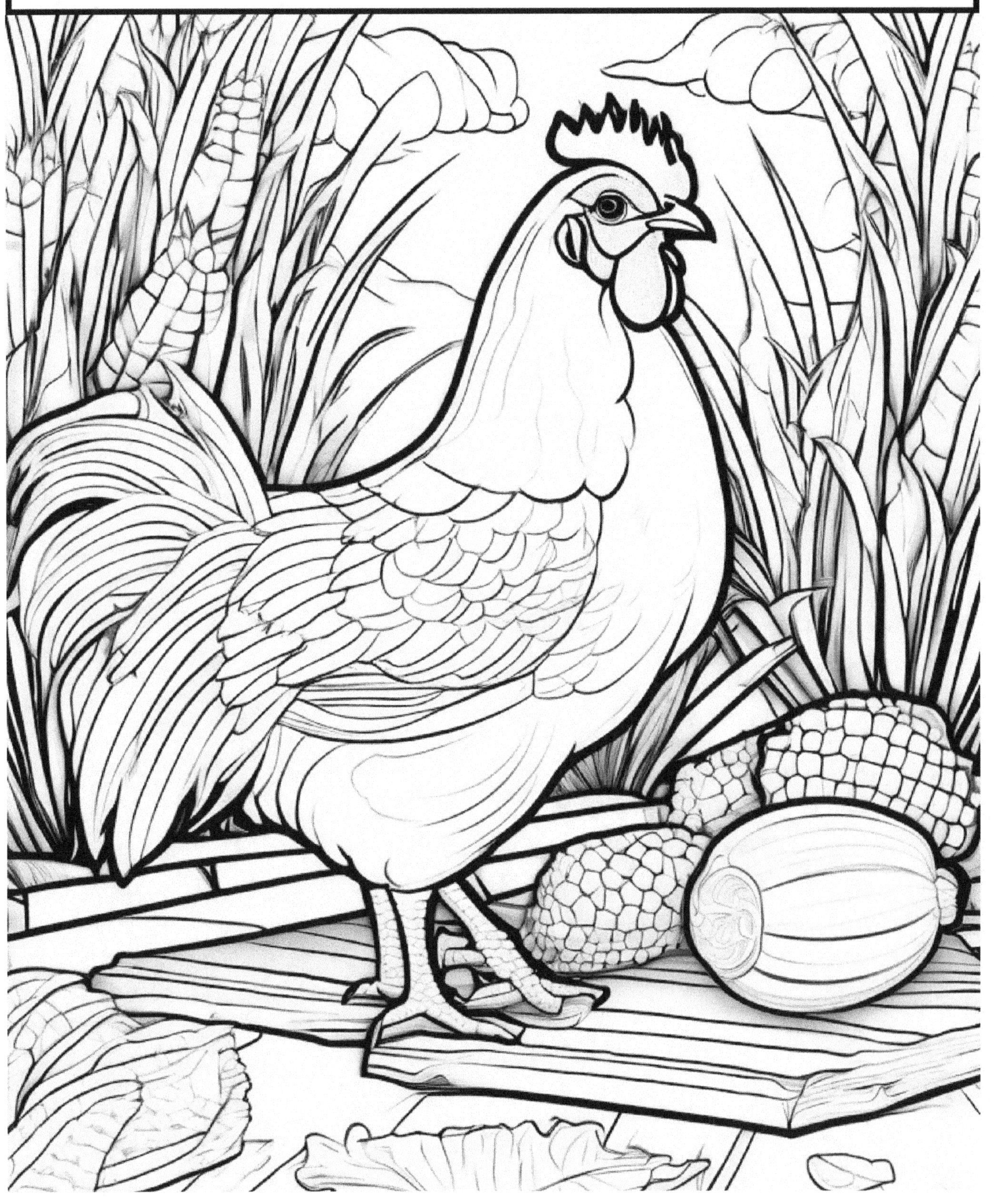

The chickens laid fresh eggs every day.

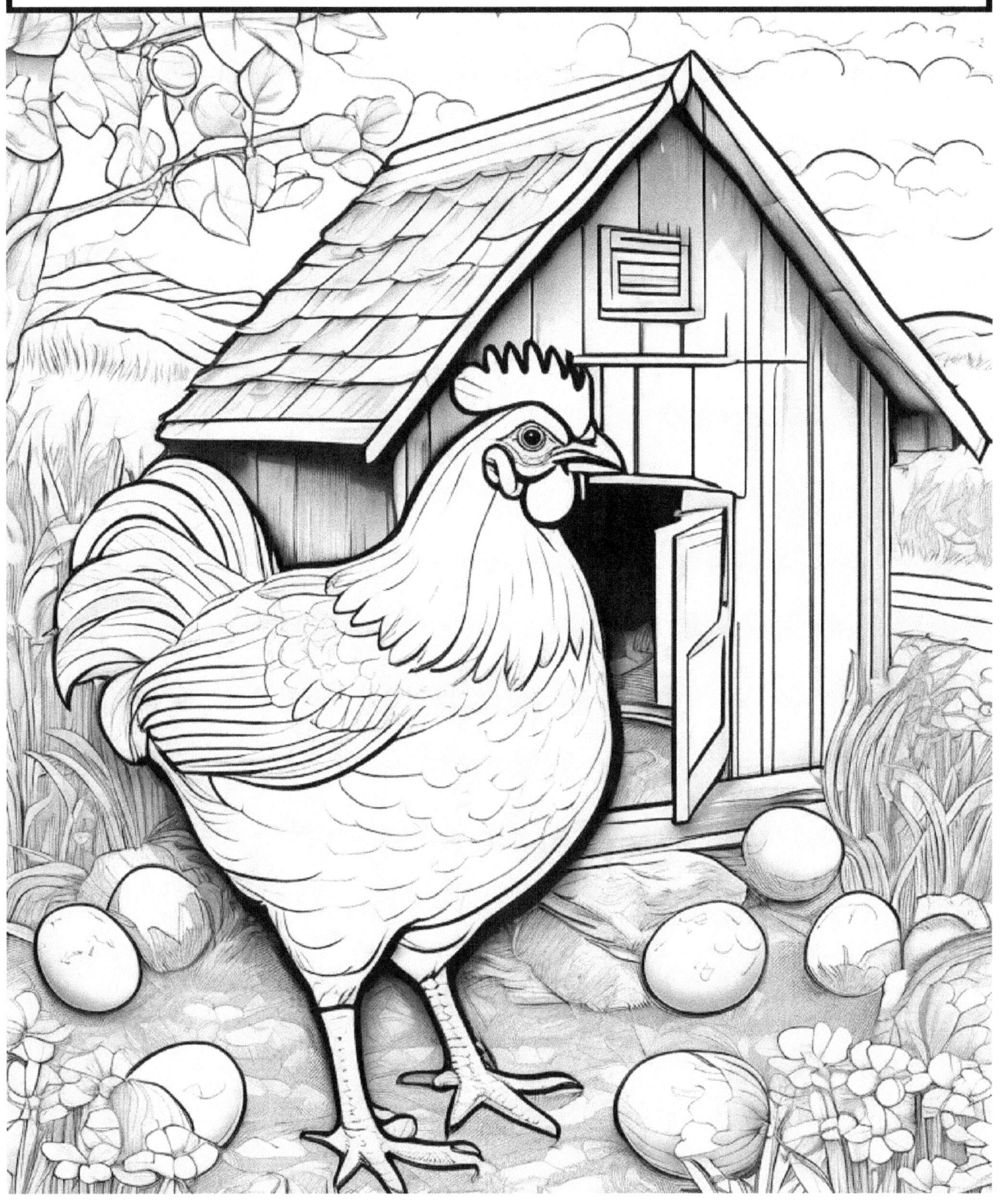

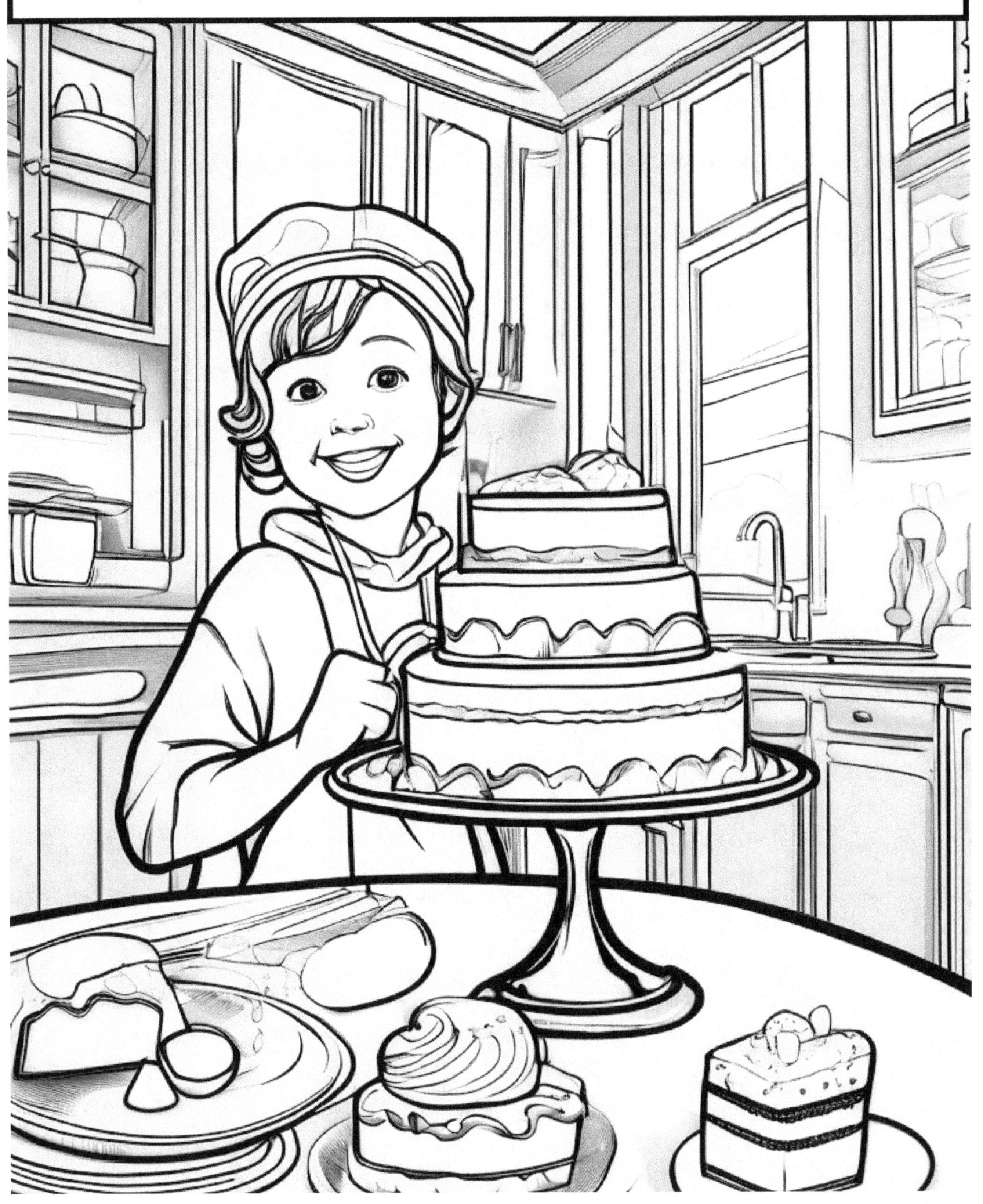

And Marcus used it to make delicious cakes.

Marcus woke up early and started his tasks on the farm.

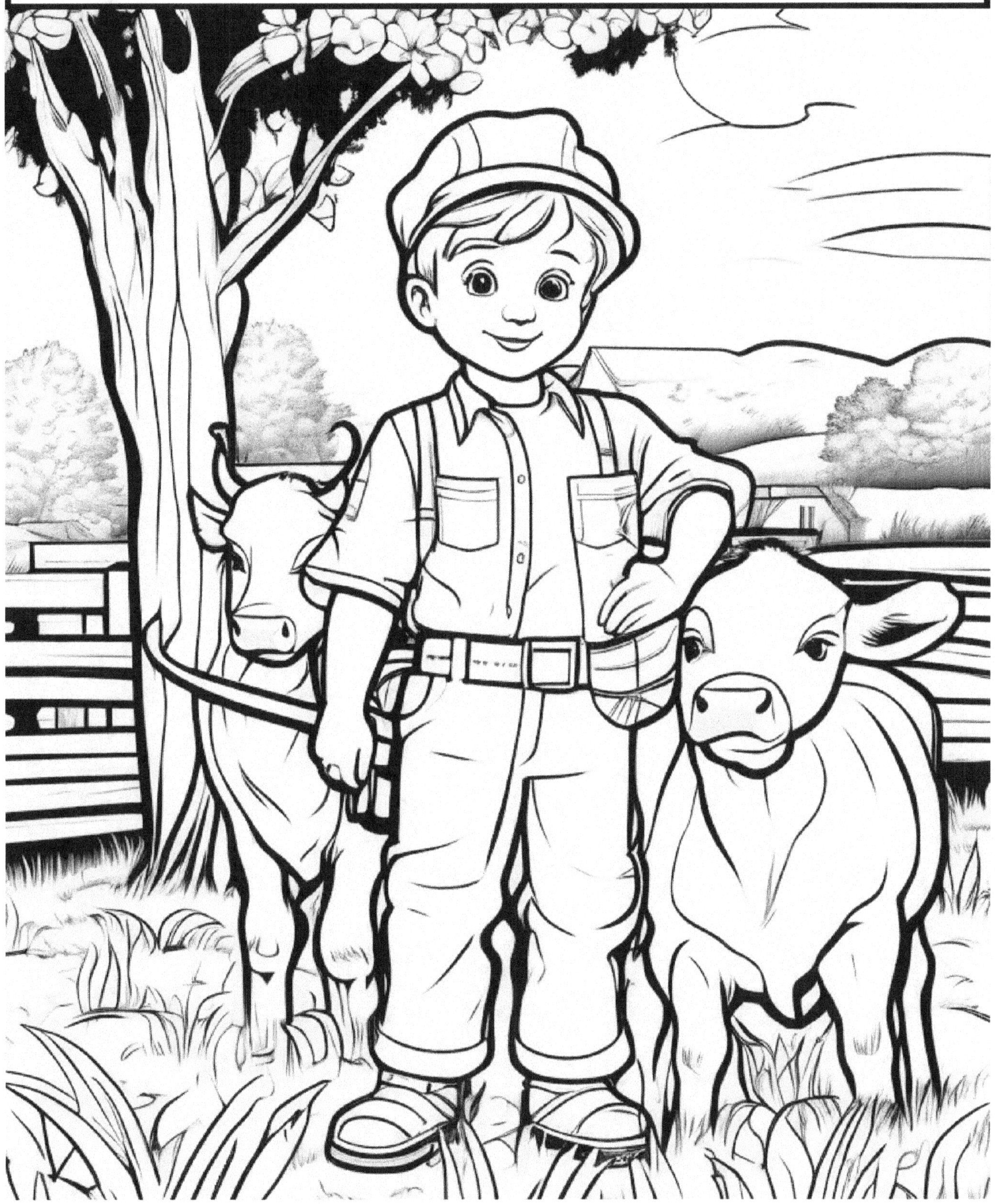

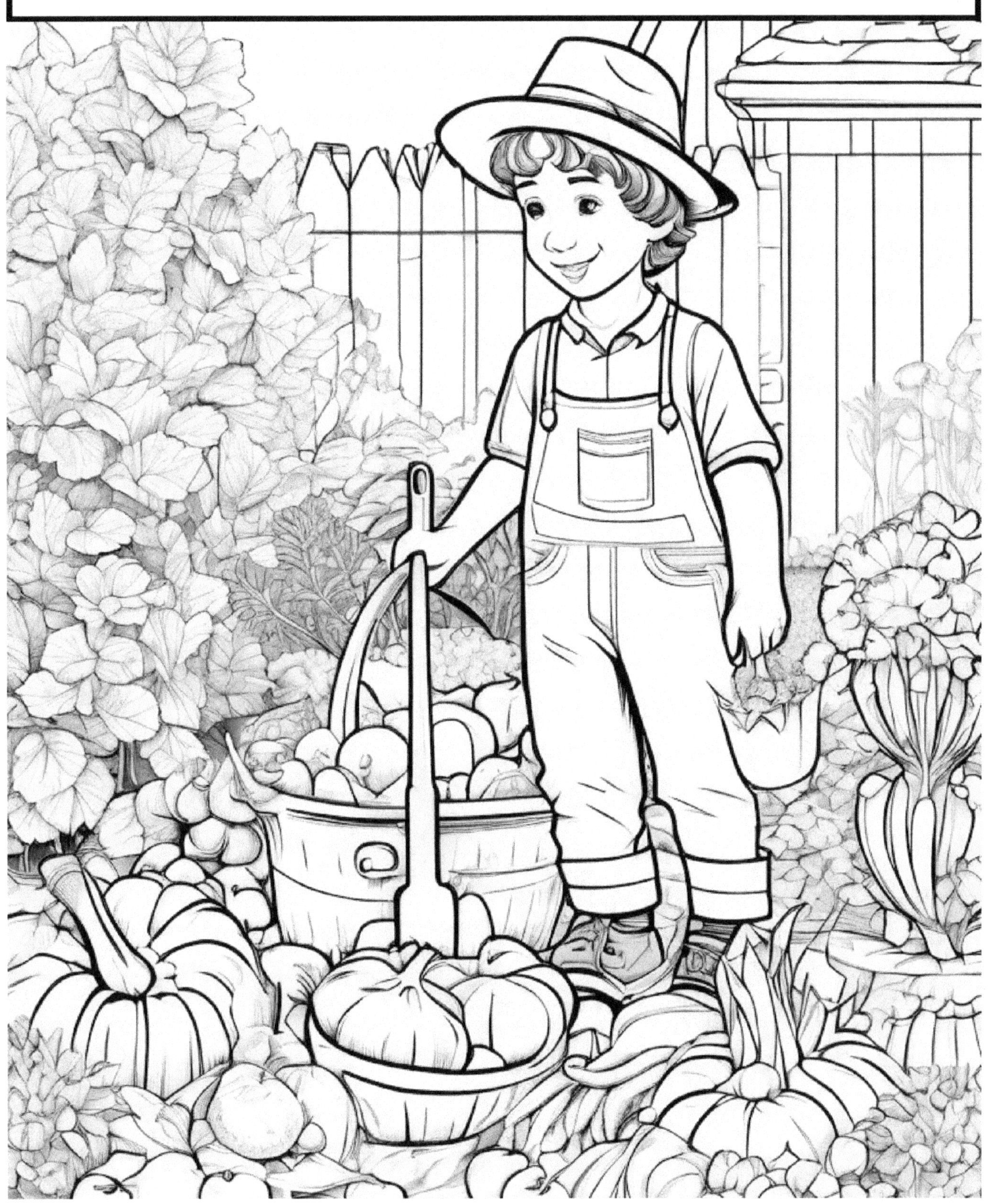
He watered the garden and harvested the ripe vegetables.

he took care of the animals with lots of love and affection.

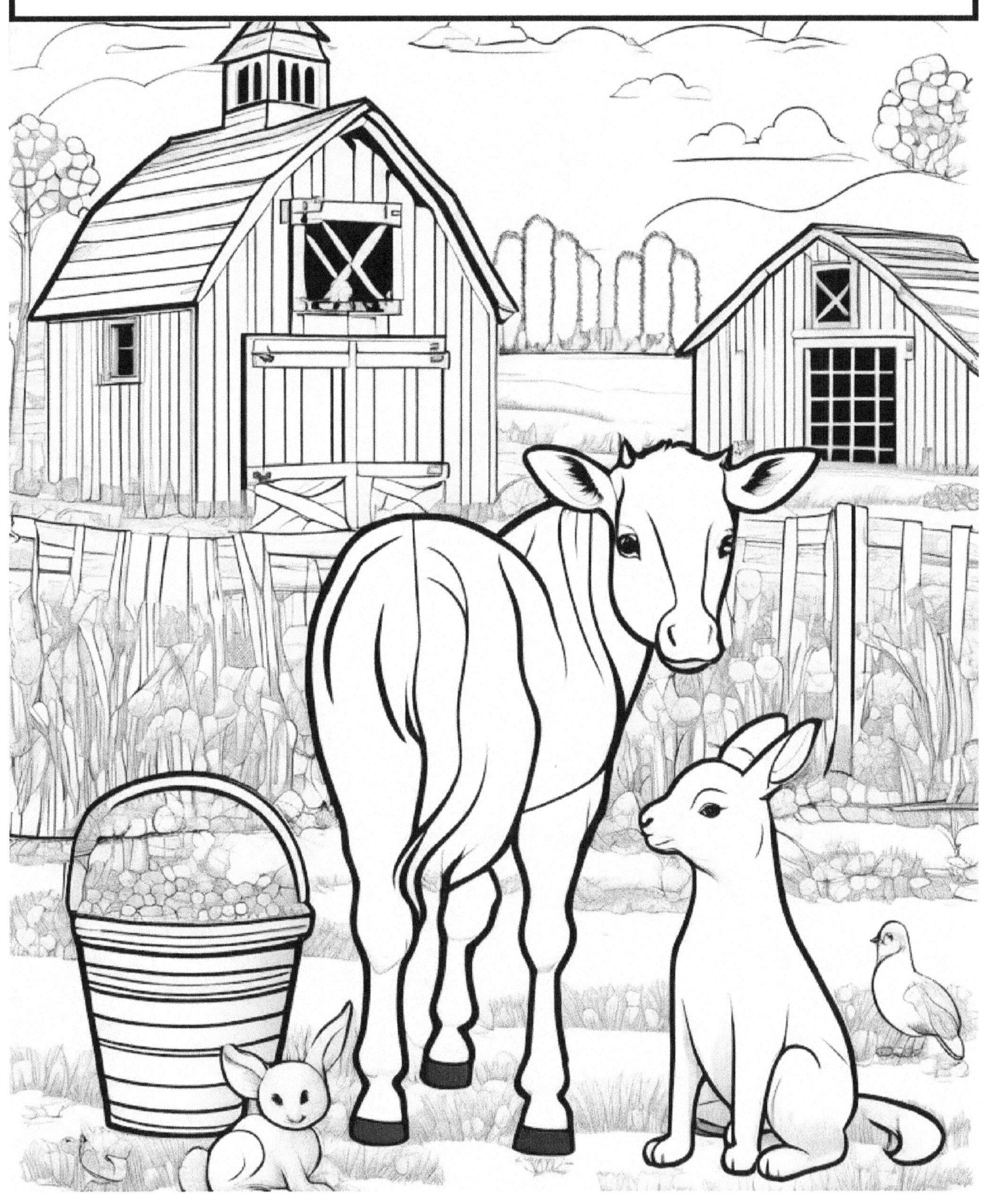

In the afternoon, Marcus invited the neighborhood children.

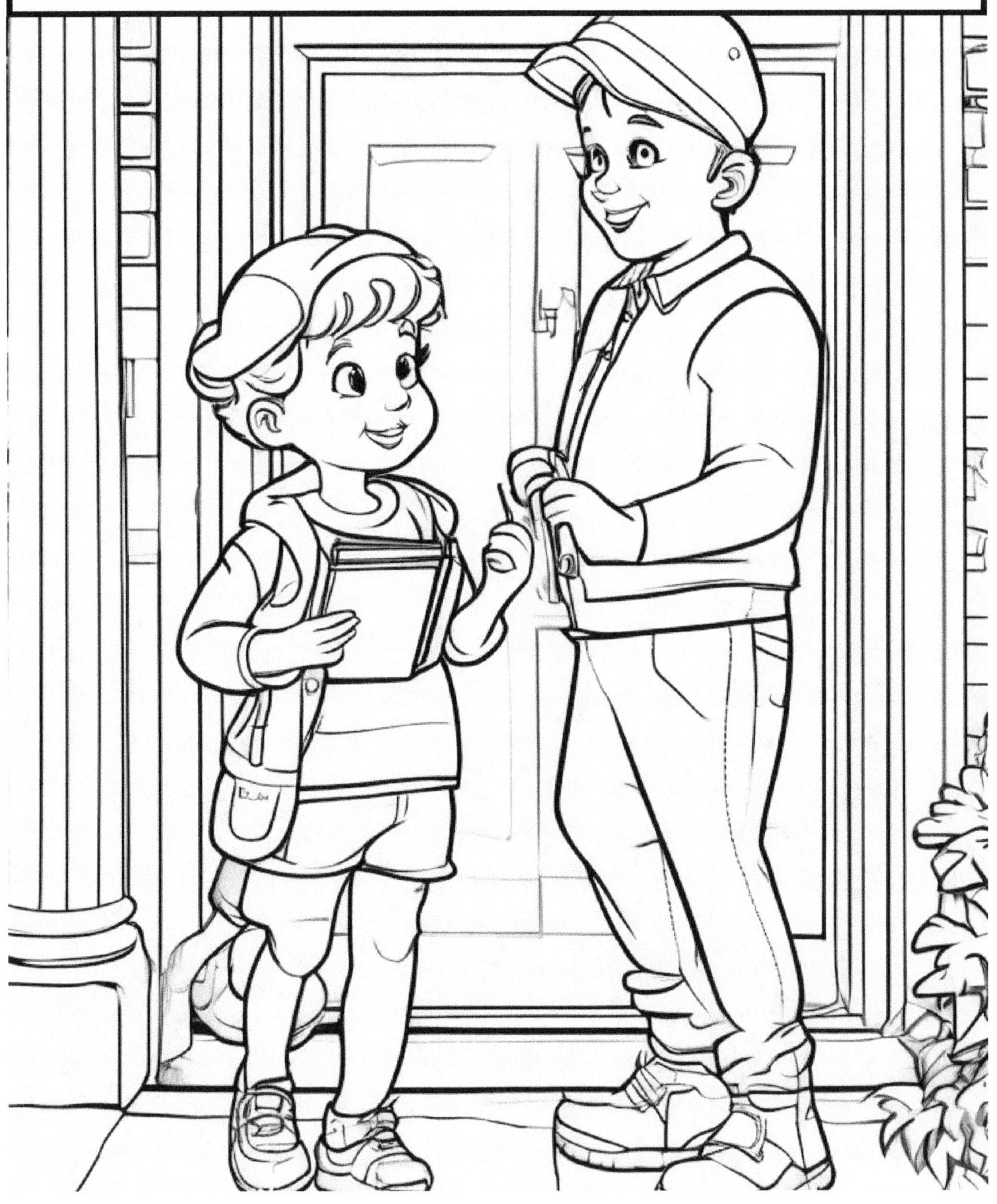

To get to know the farm and learn about nature.

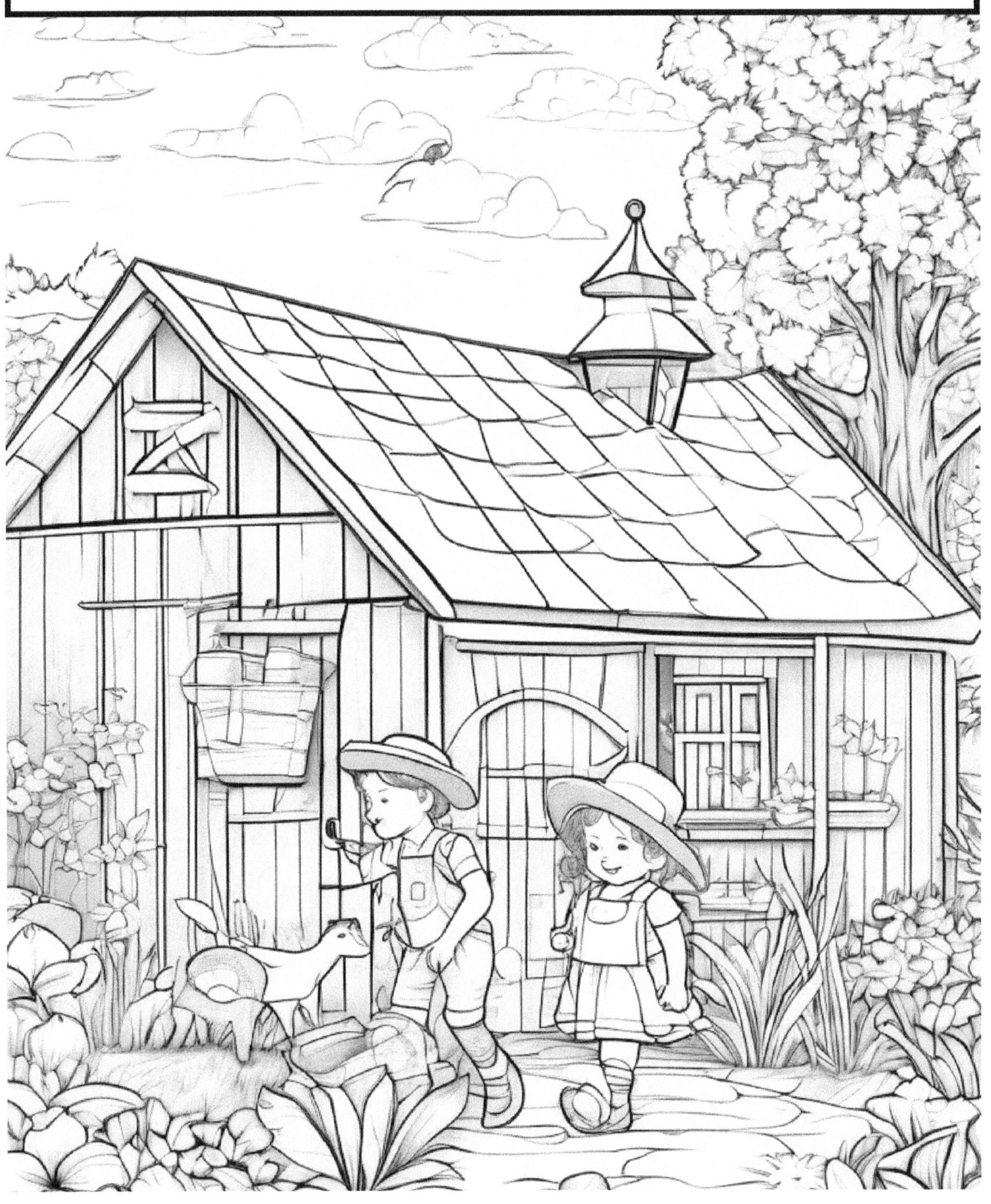

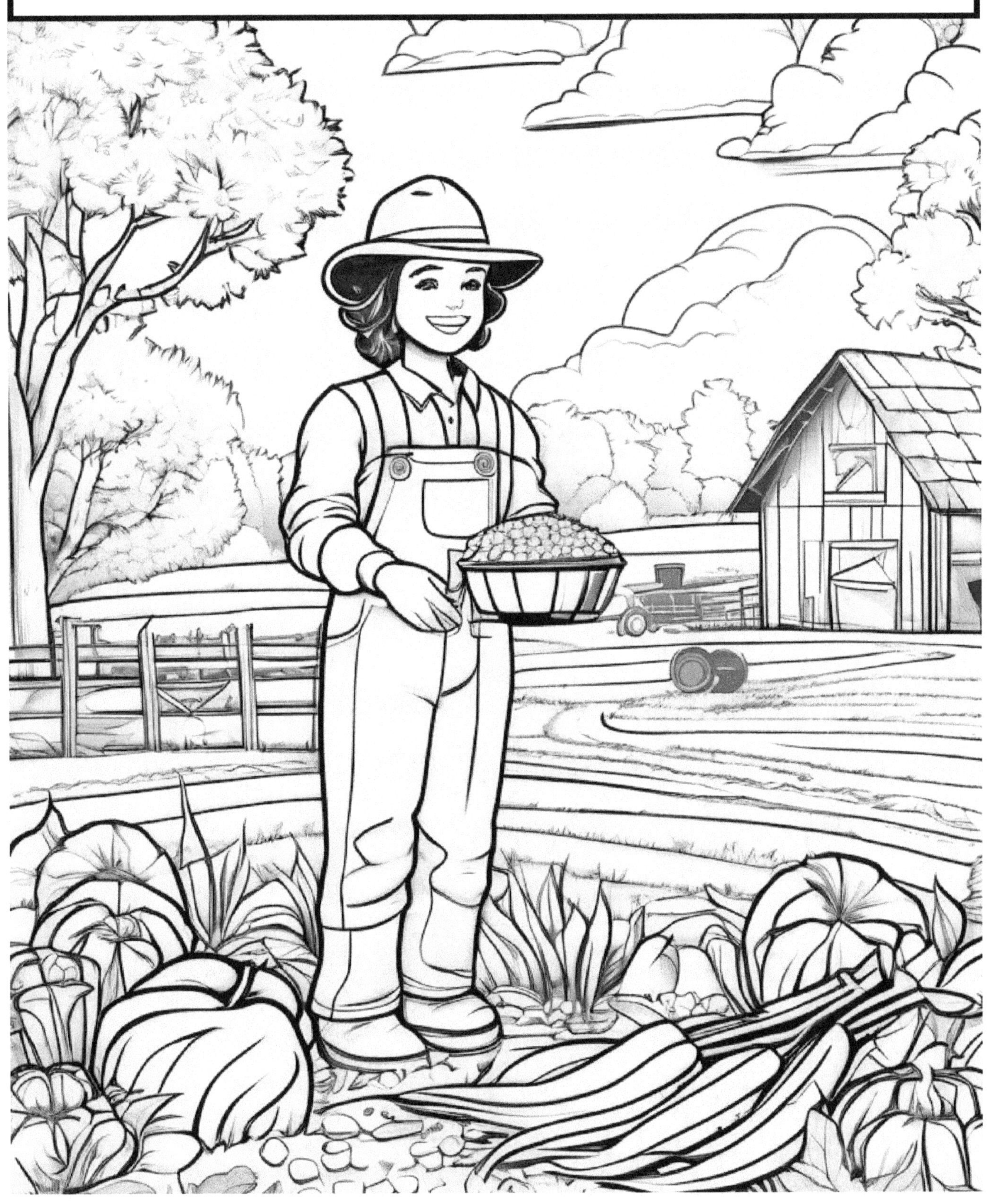
Marcus showed the children how to plant seeds.

And how to water the seedlings so that they grow healthy.

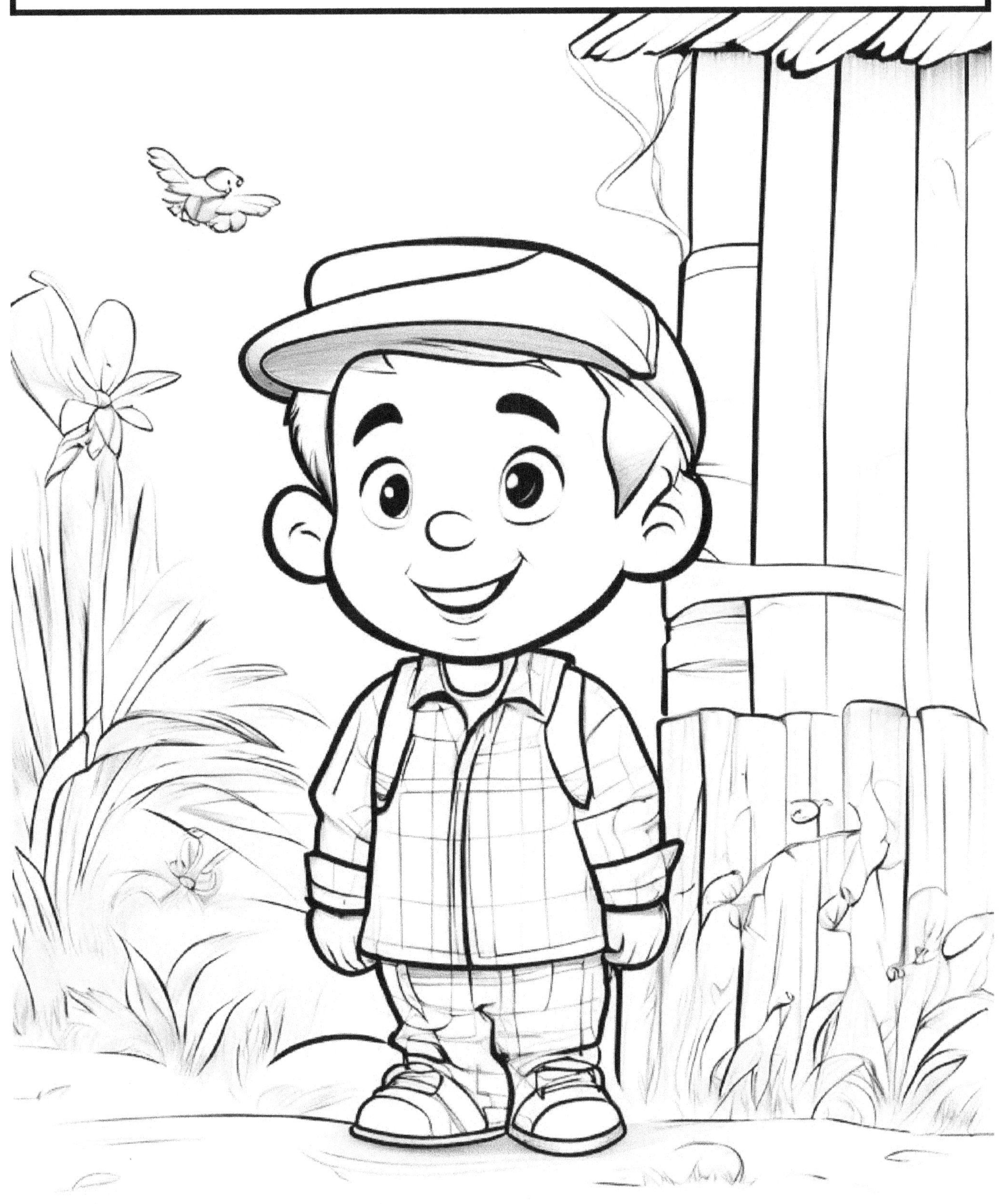

He explained the importance of respecting the land and animals.

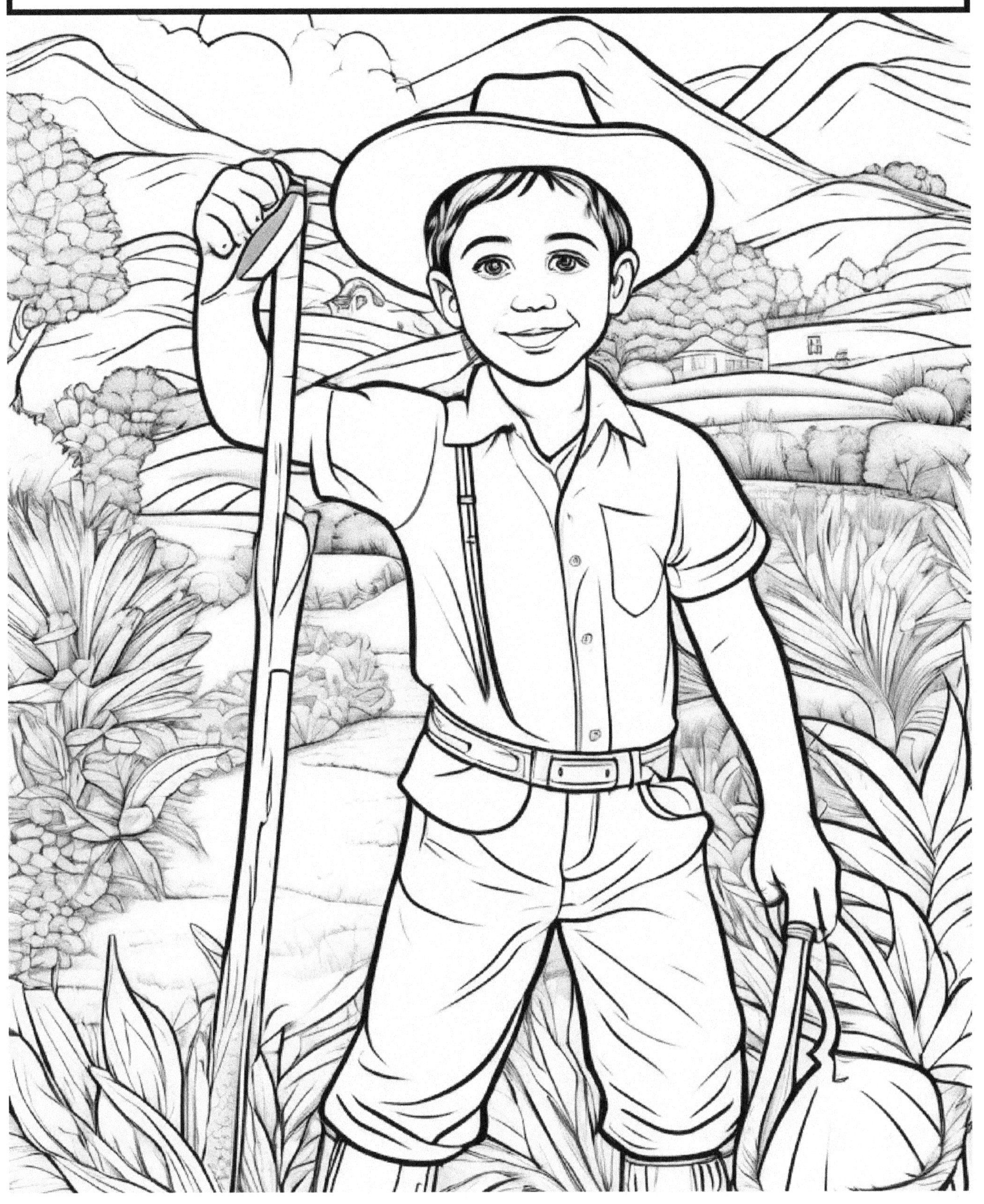

And on his farm there is a pond full of different types of fish

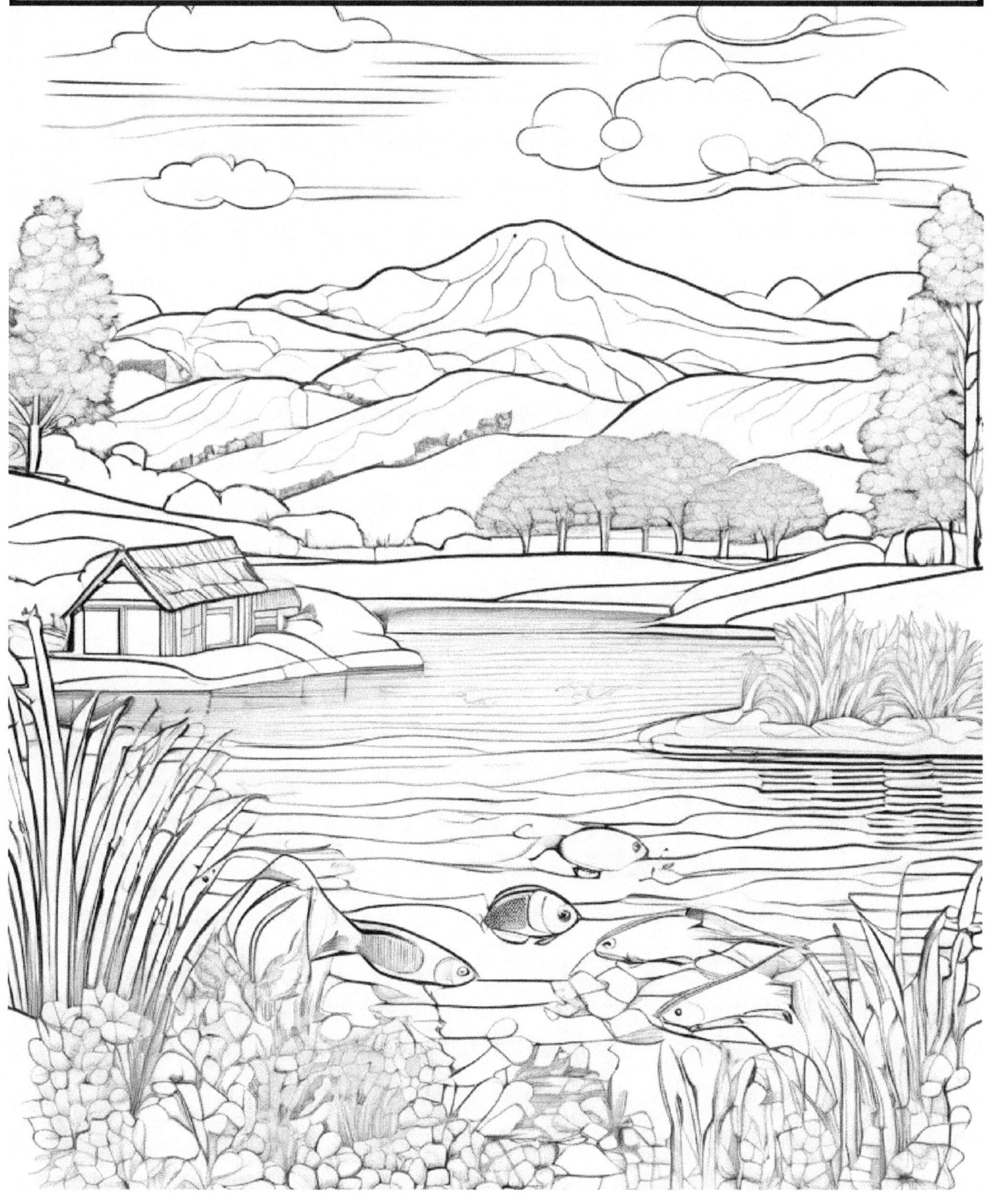

As the children explored the farm.

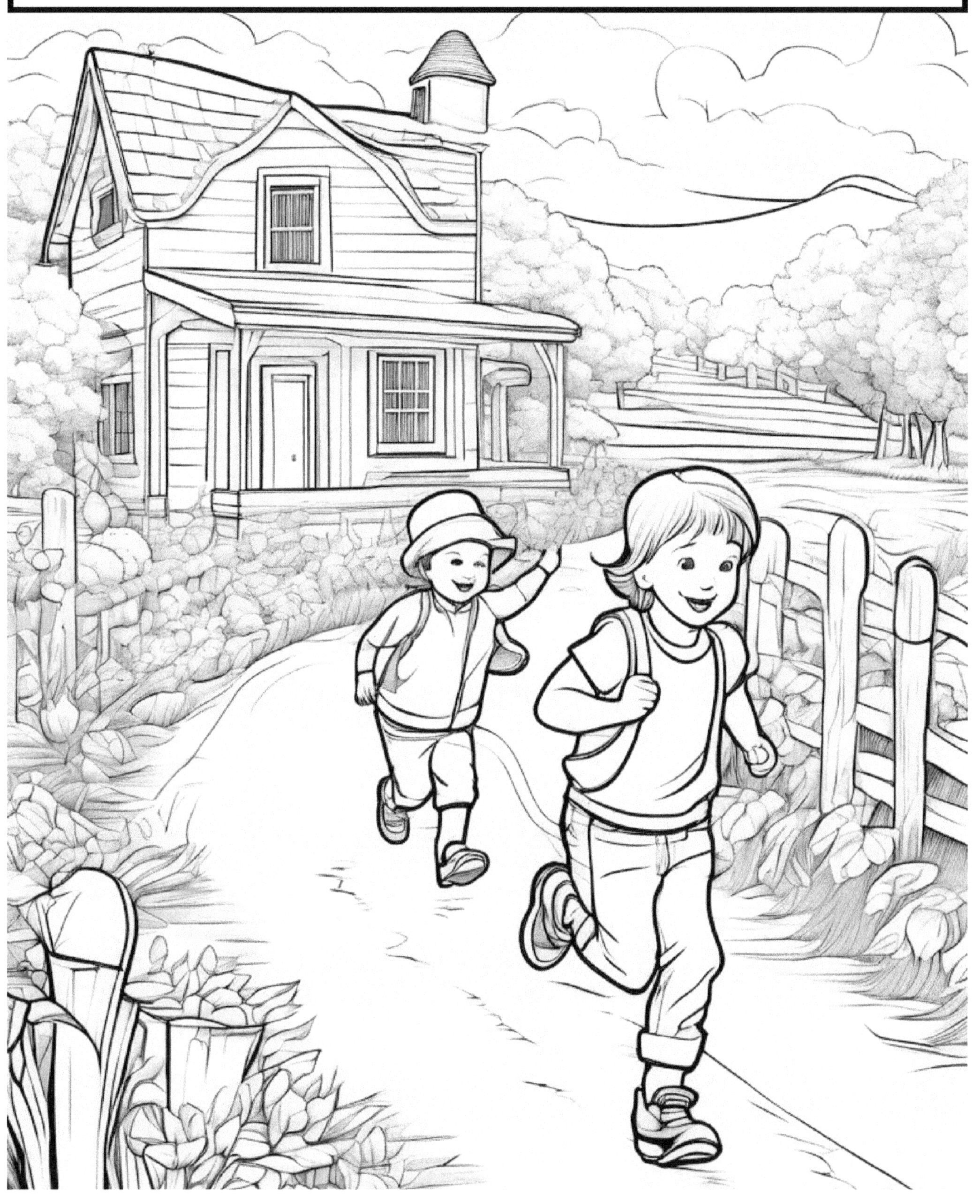

The children were delighted to see the vegetables
and animals.

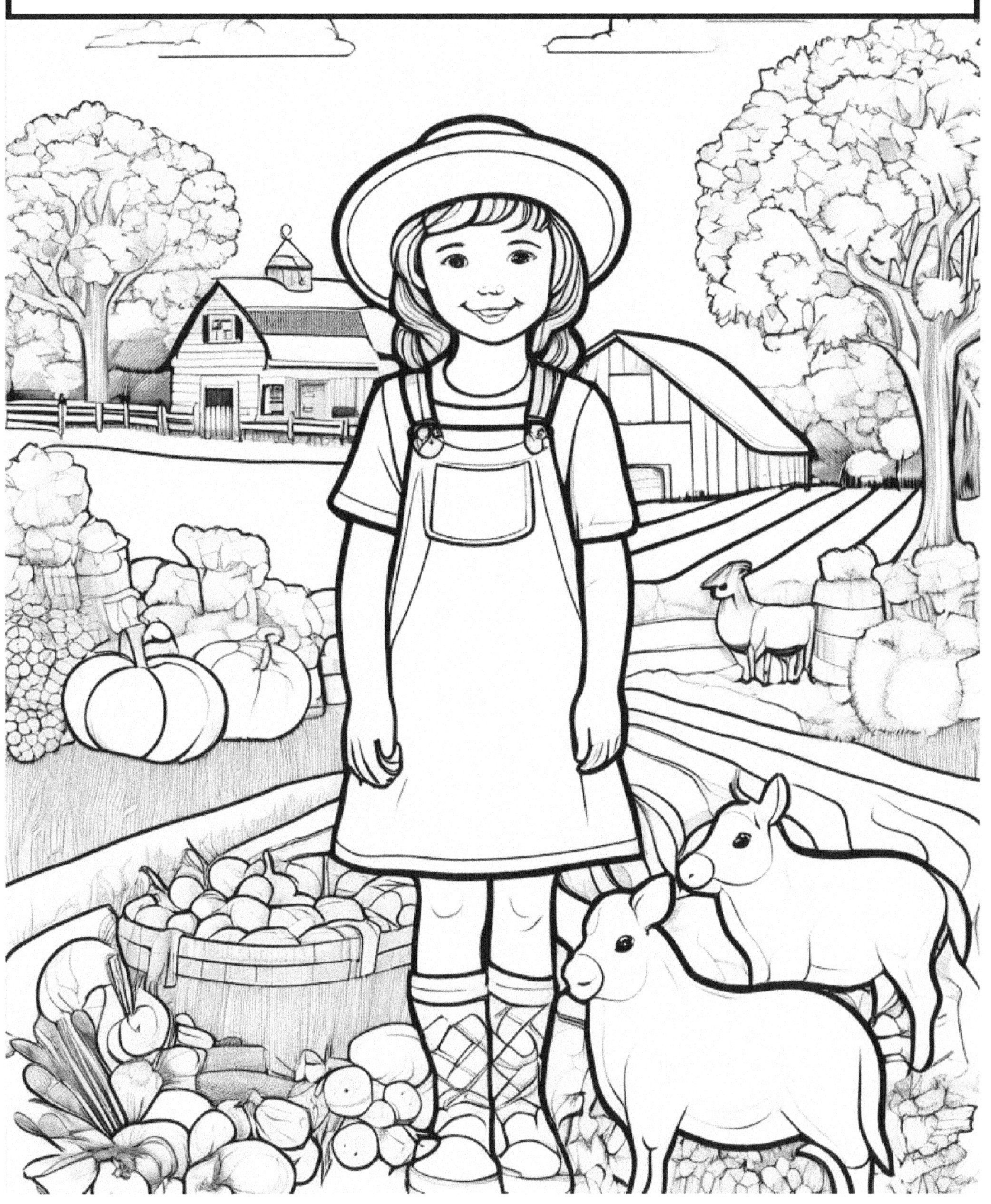

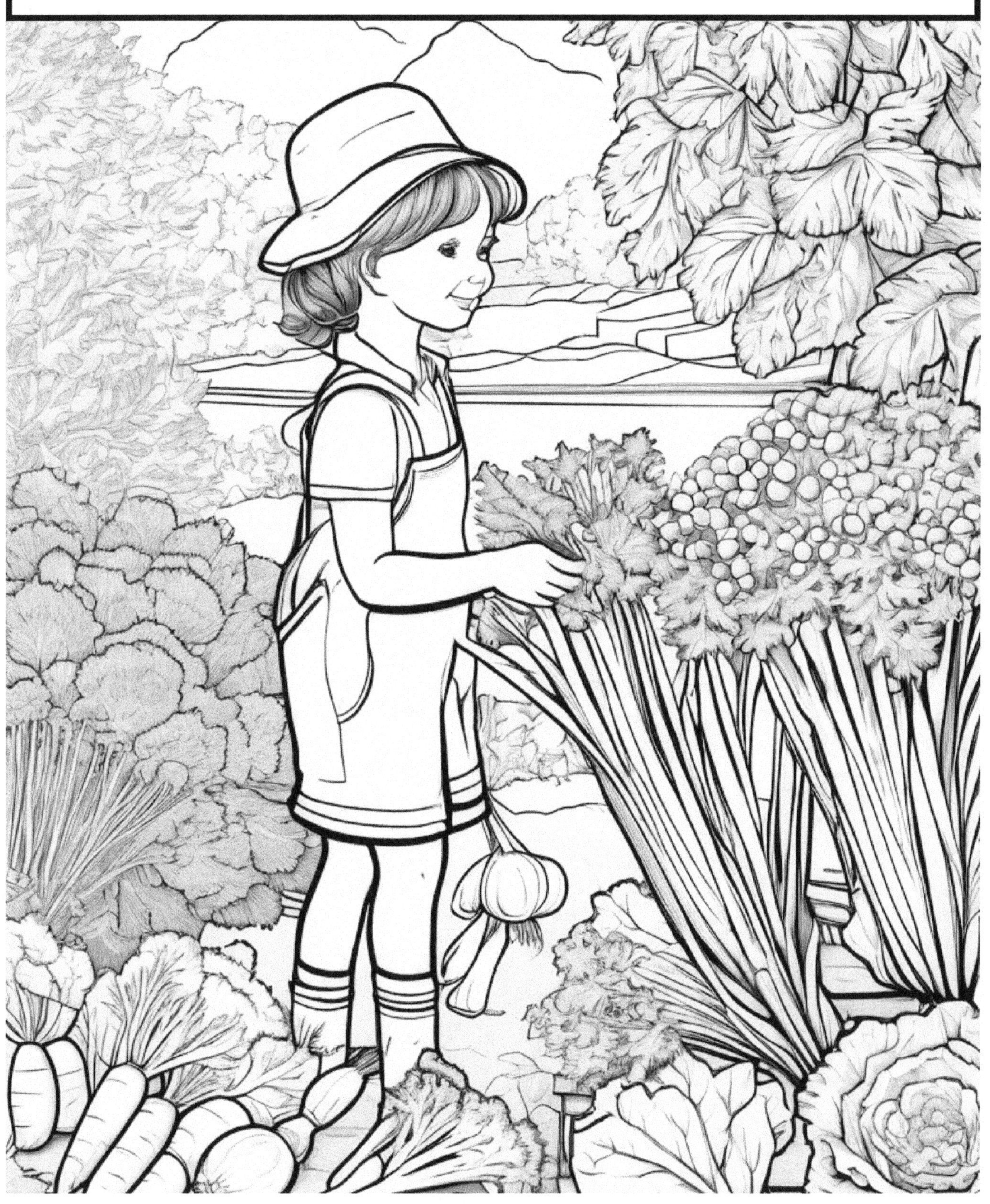

Some children helped harvest carrots and lettuce.

Other children rode the Lightning horse.

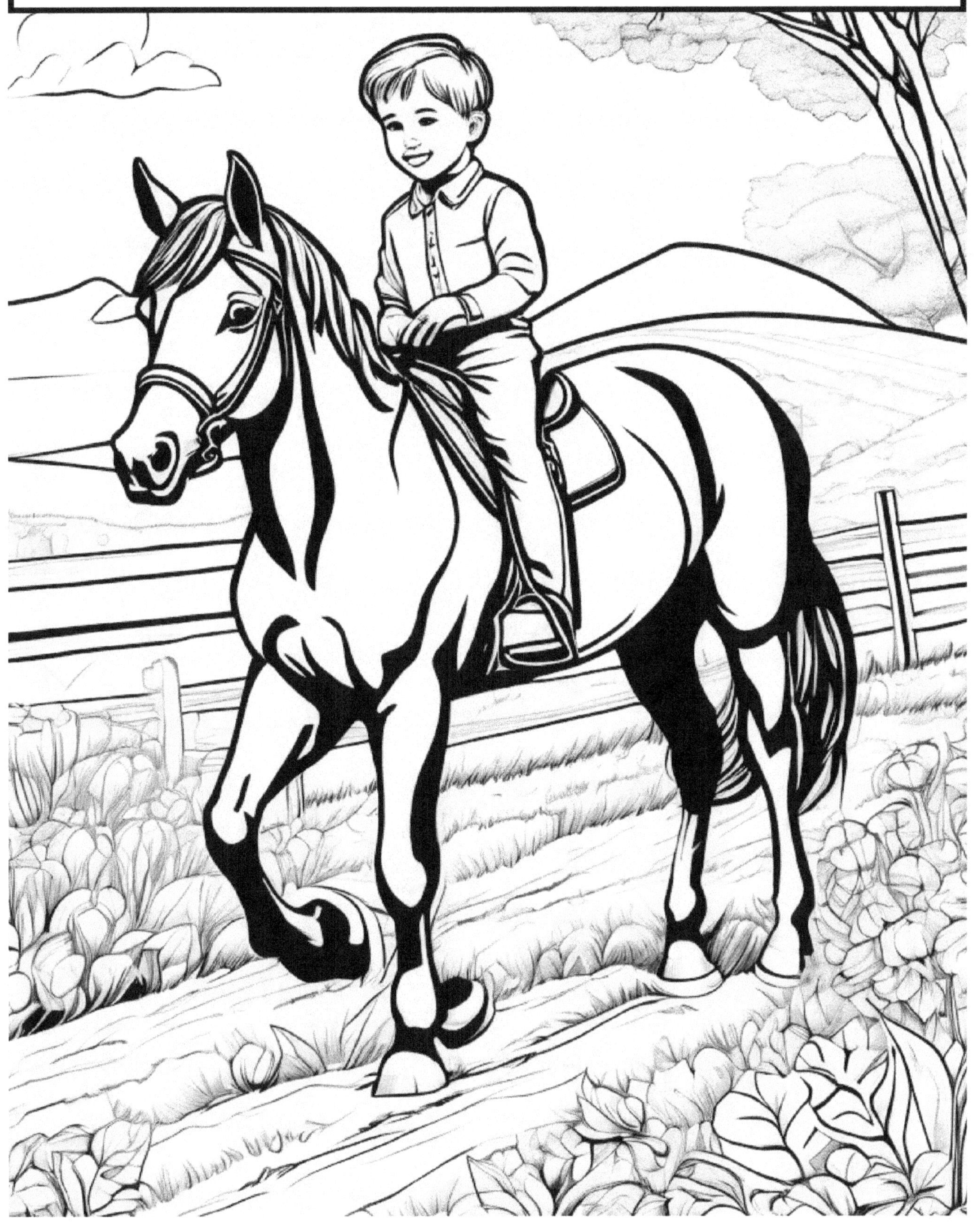

For a fun walk around the farm.

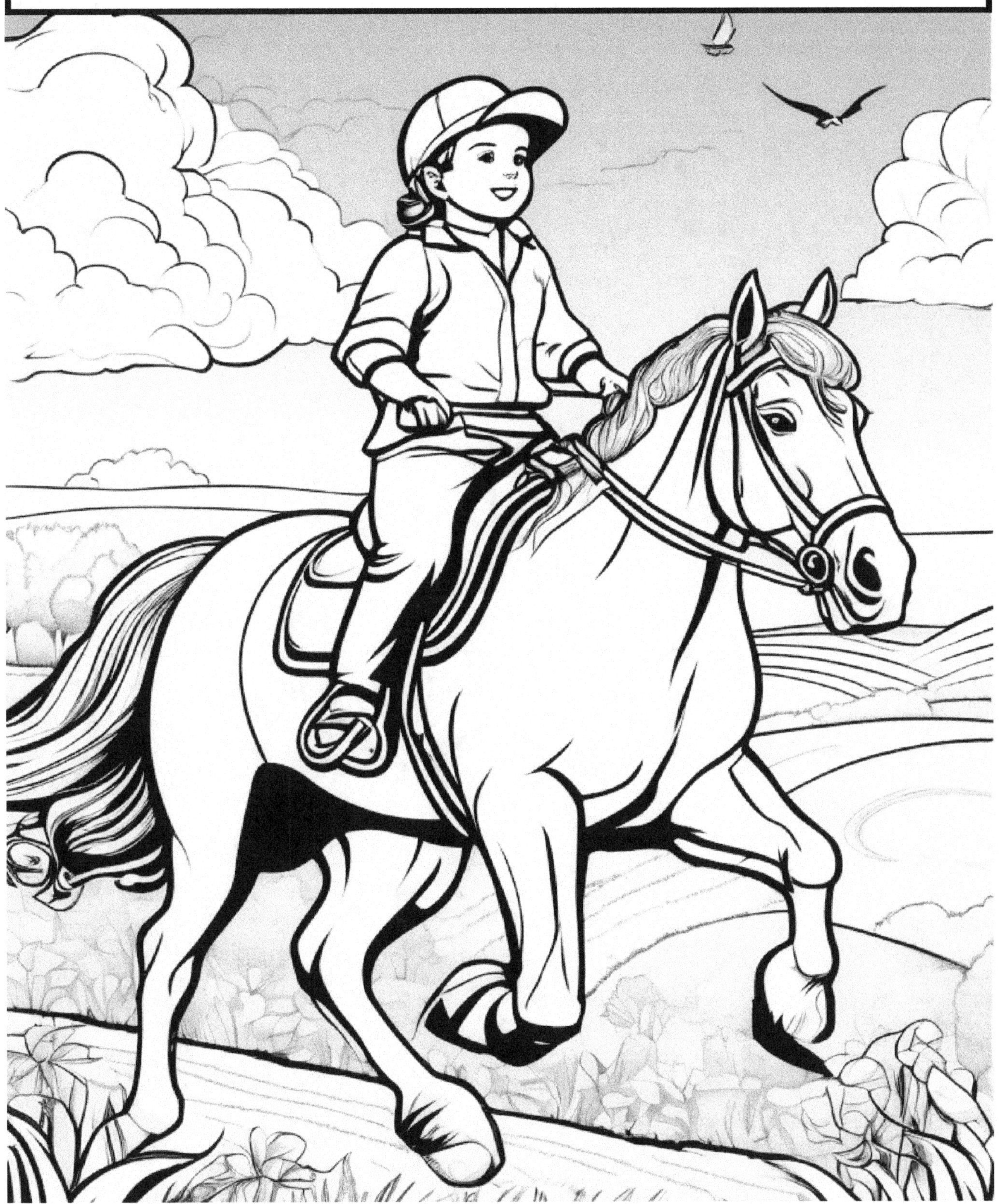

Marcus taught about the life cycles of animals.

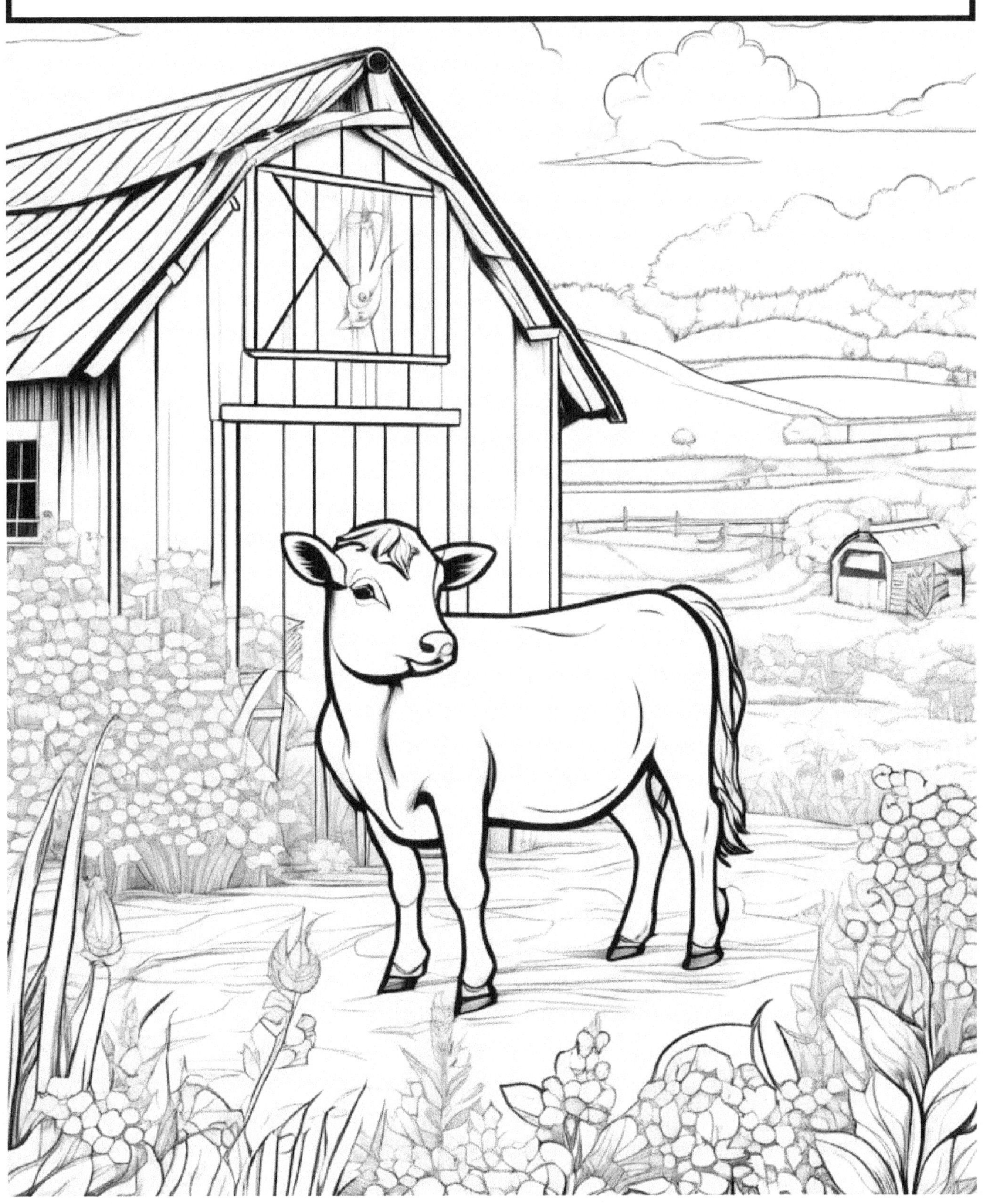

How the chicks hatched from the eggs and grew strong.

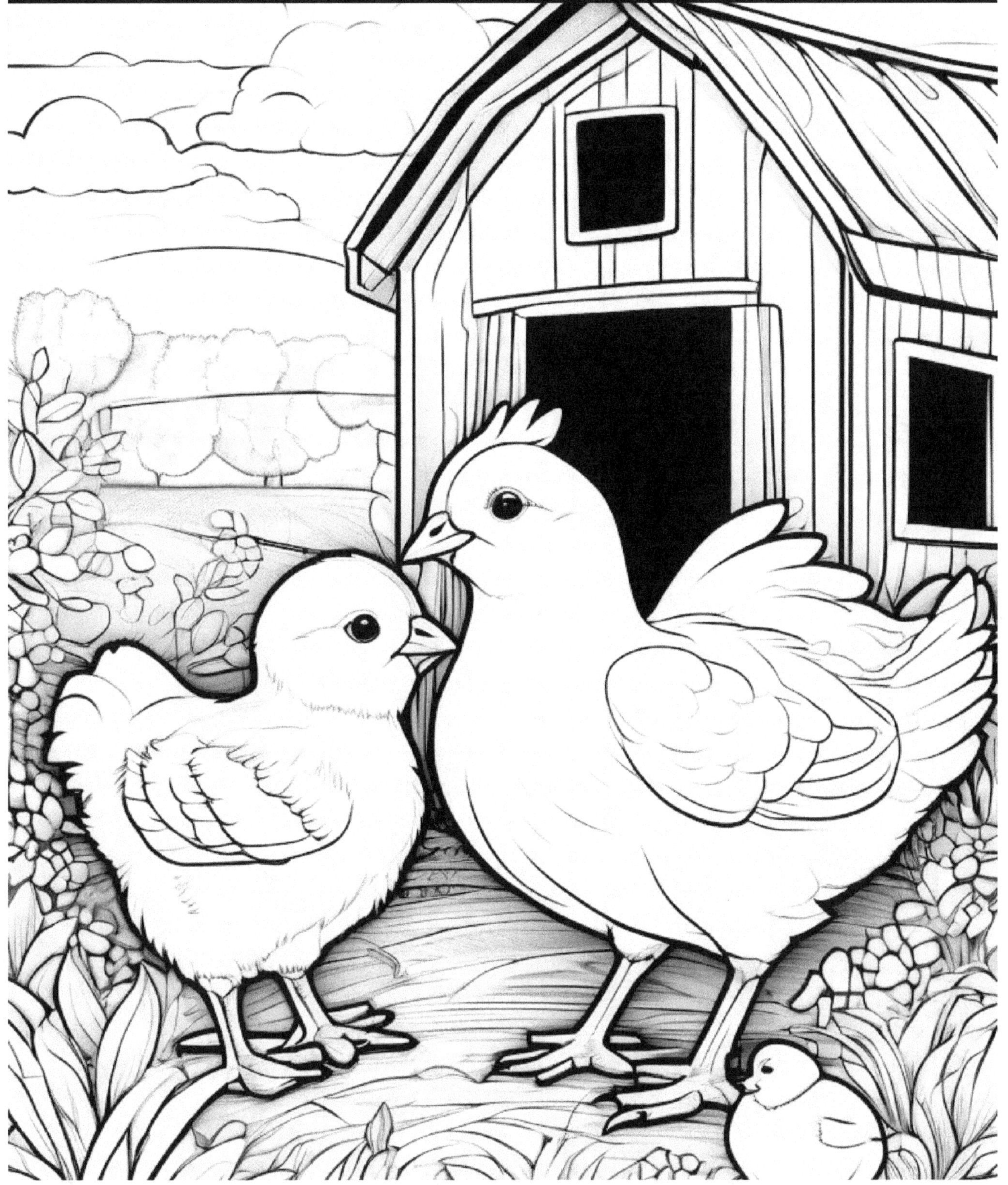

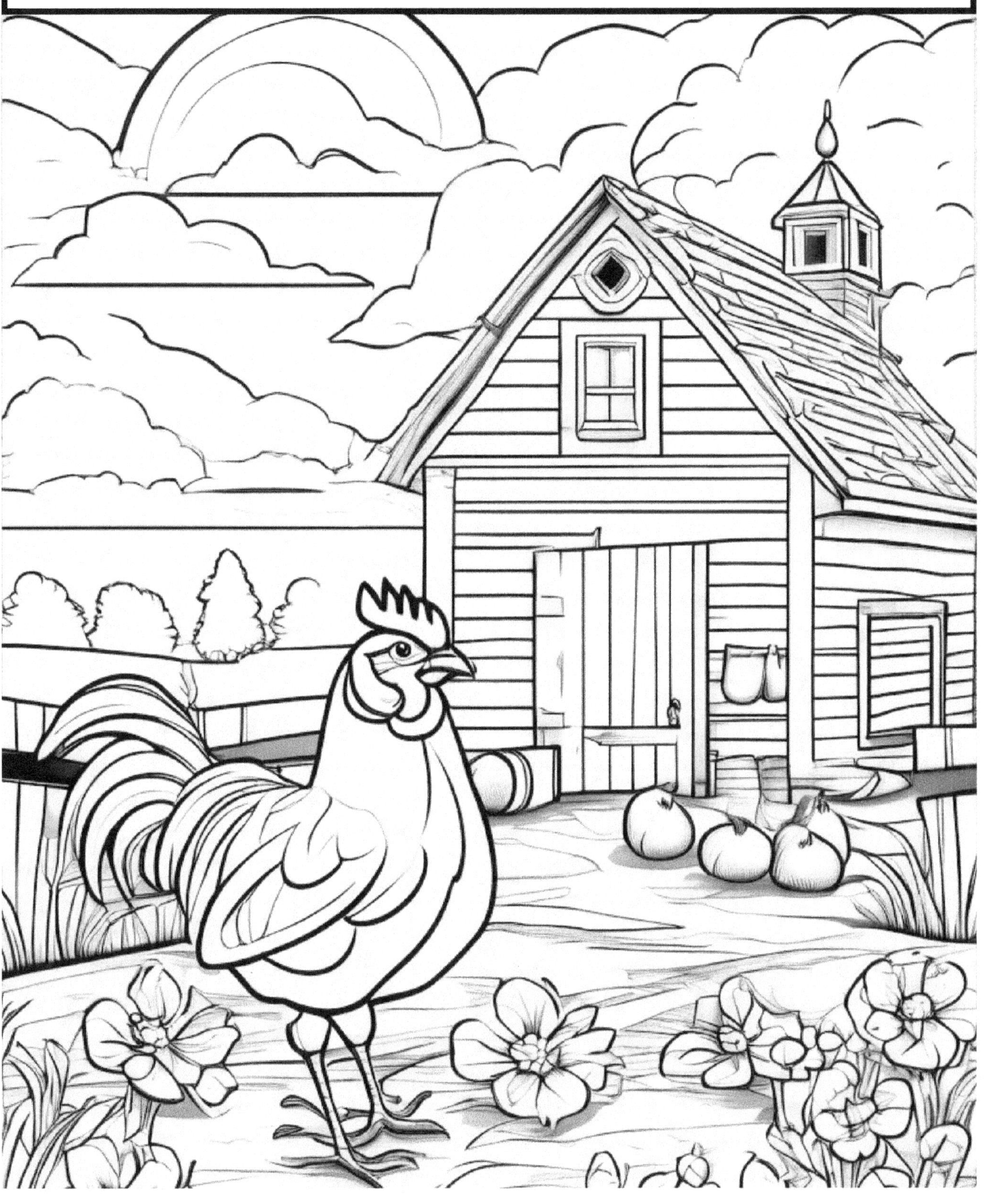
And how they turned into strong chickens.

Marcus talked about taking care of the environment and preserving it.

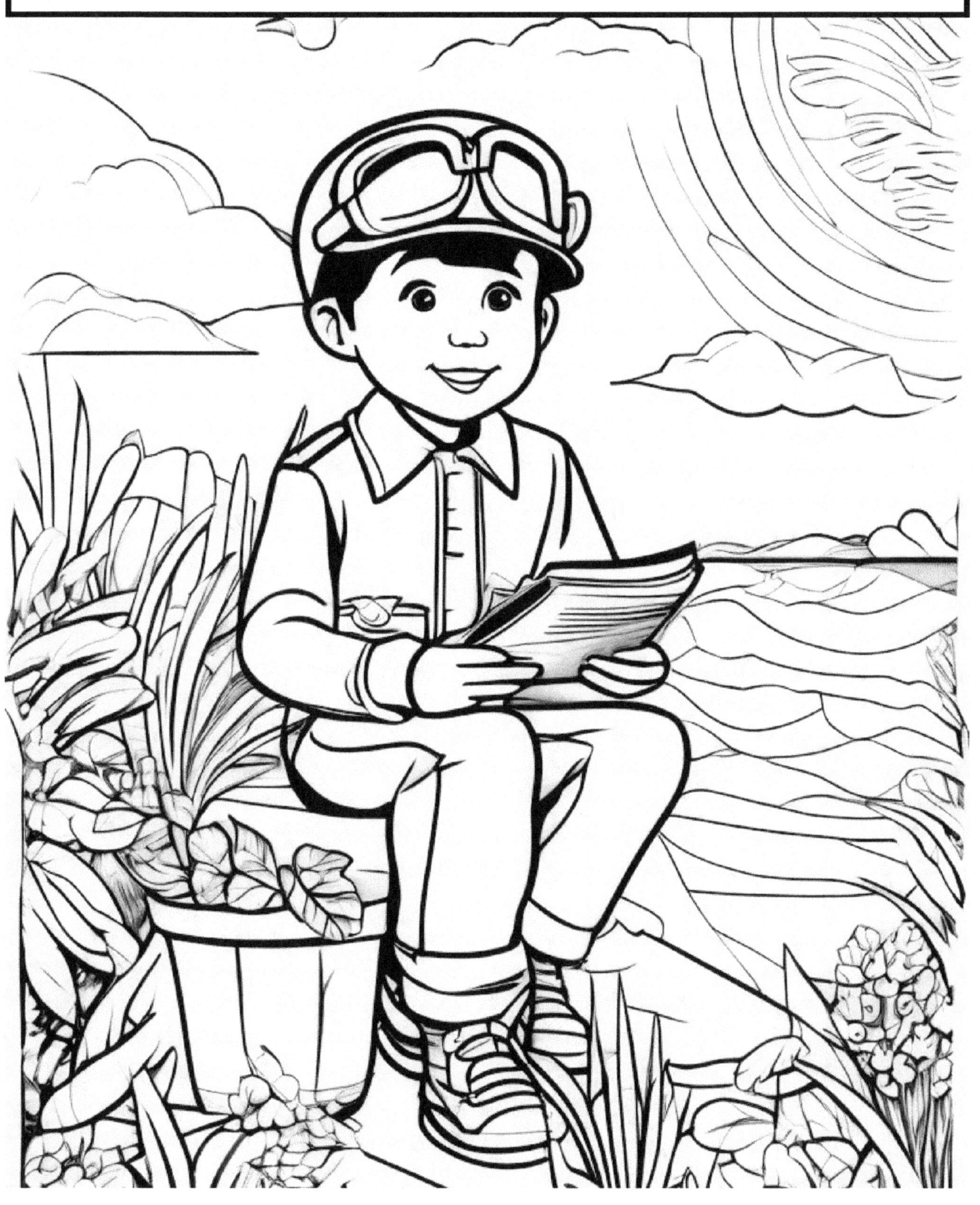

Marcus recycles trash and preserves nature.

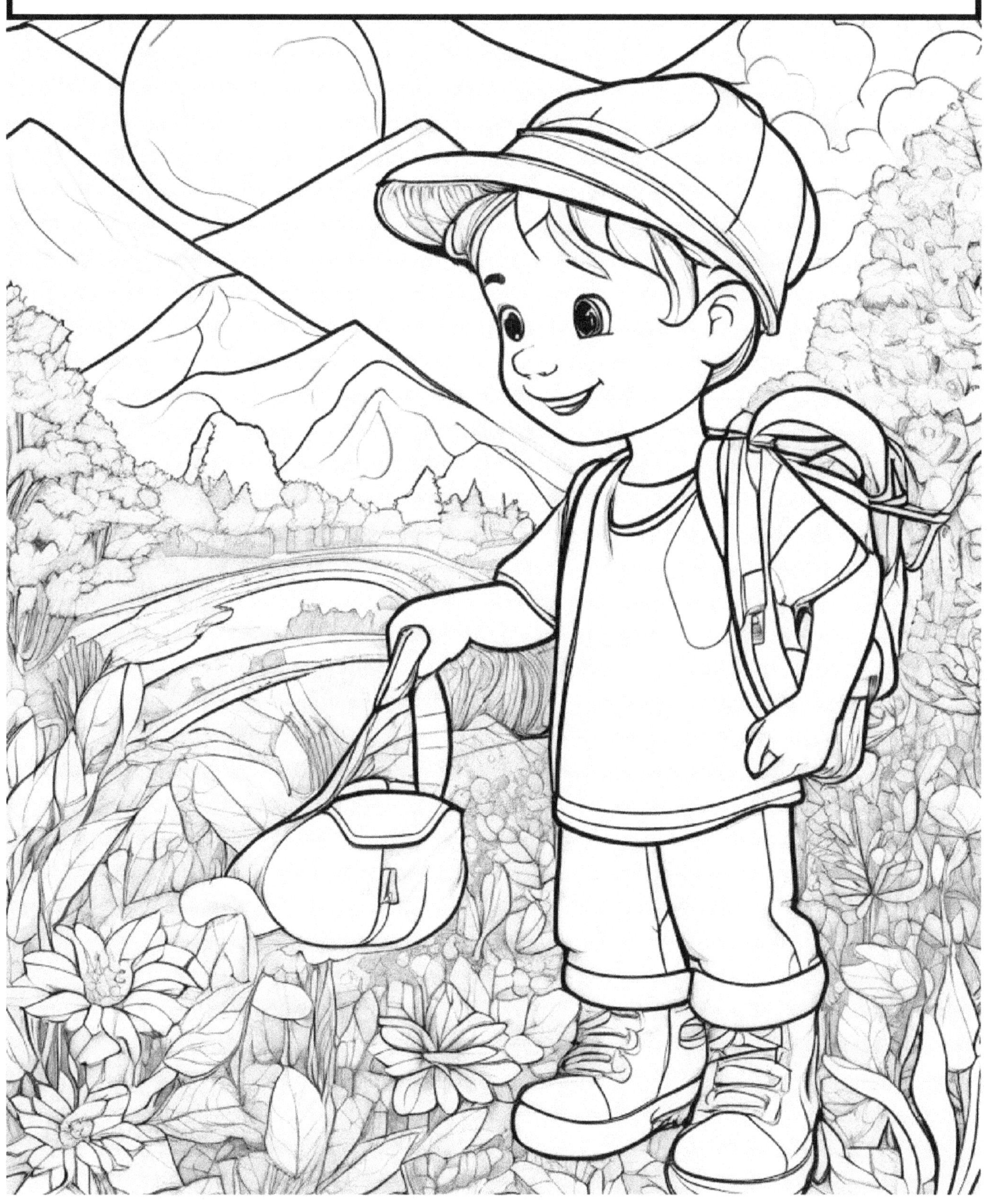

At the end of the day, Marcus felt happy and
fulfilled.

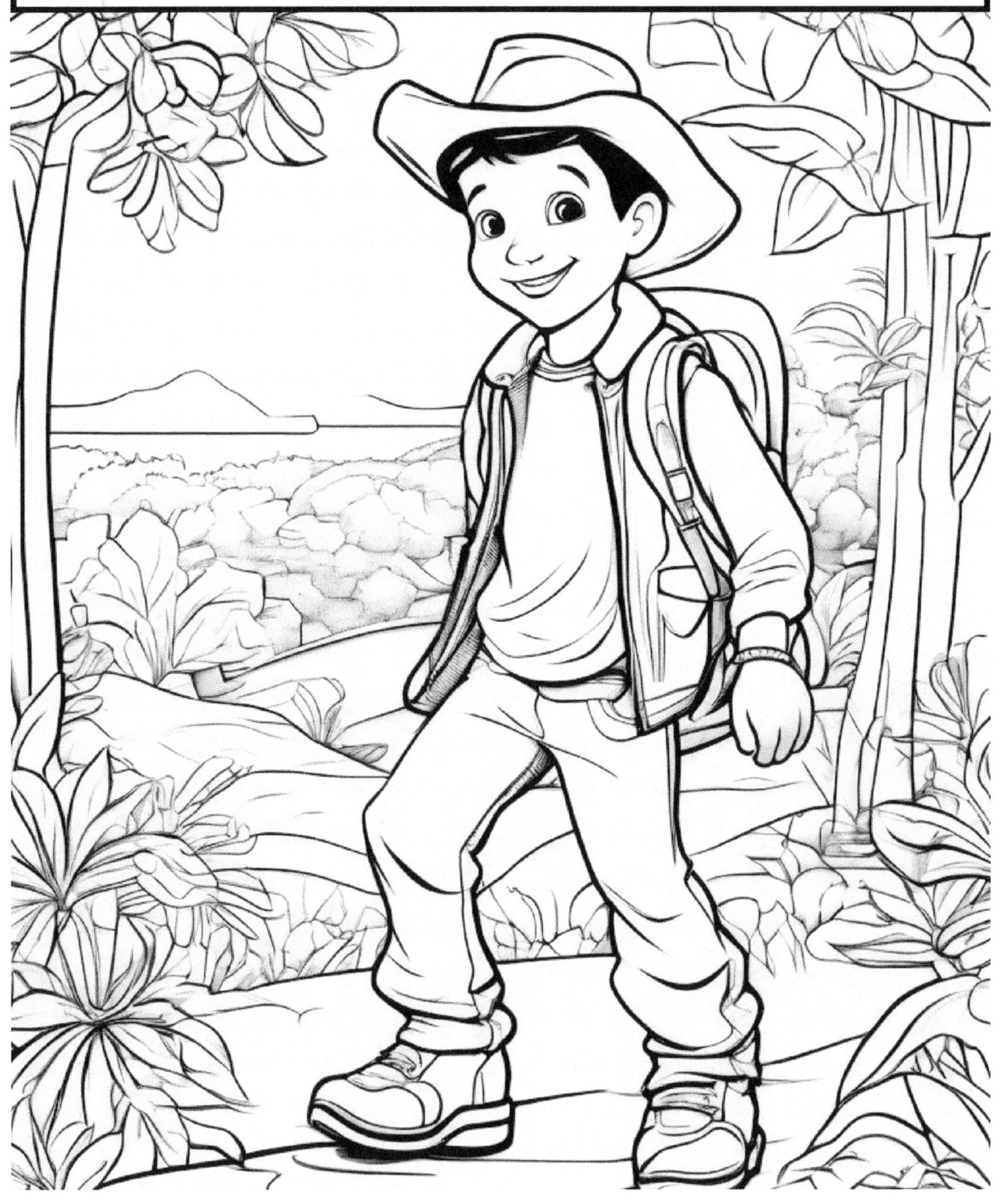

Marcus looked at his farm full of crops.

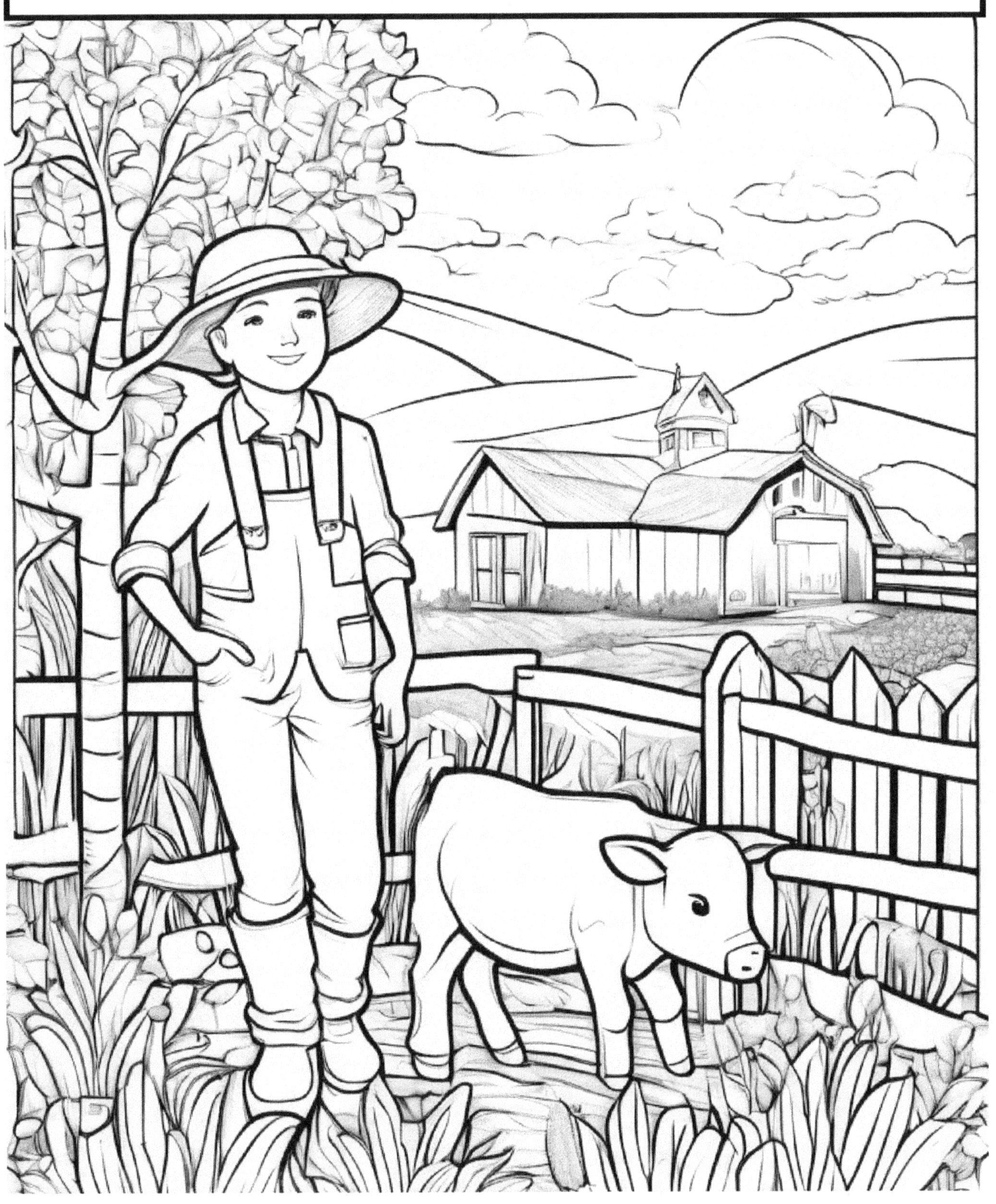

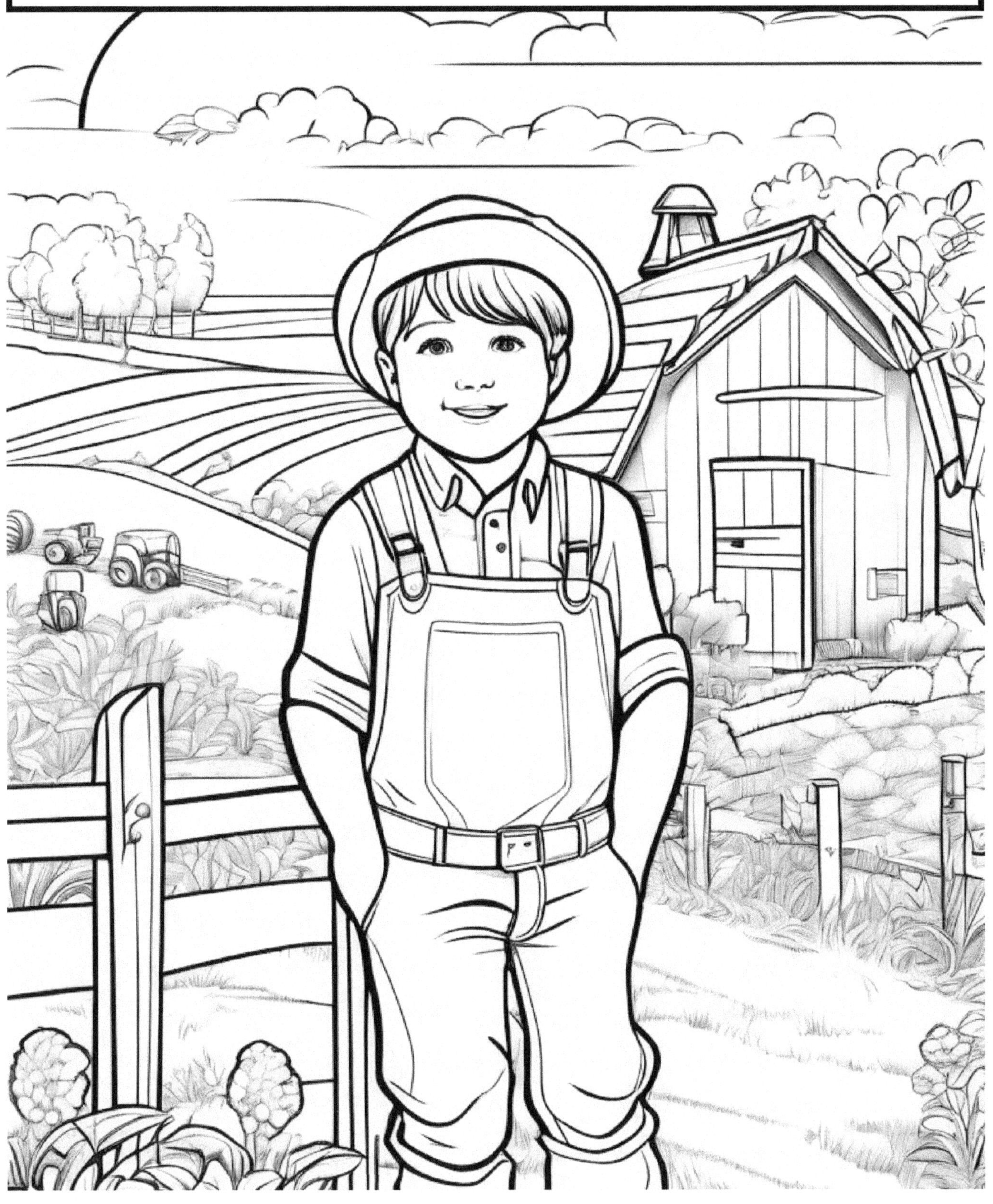

And contemplate the beauty of nature in every corner

Marcus knew what his day-to-day job was.

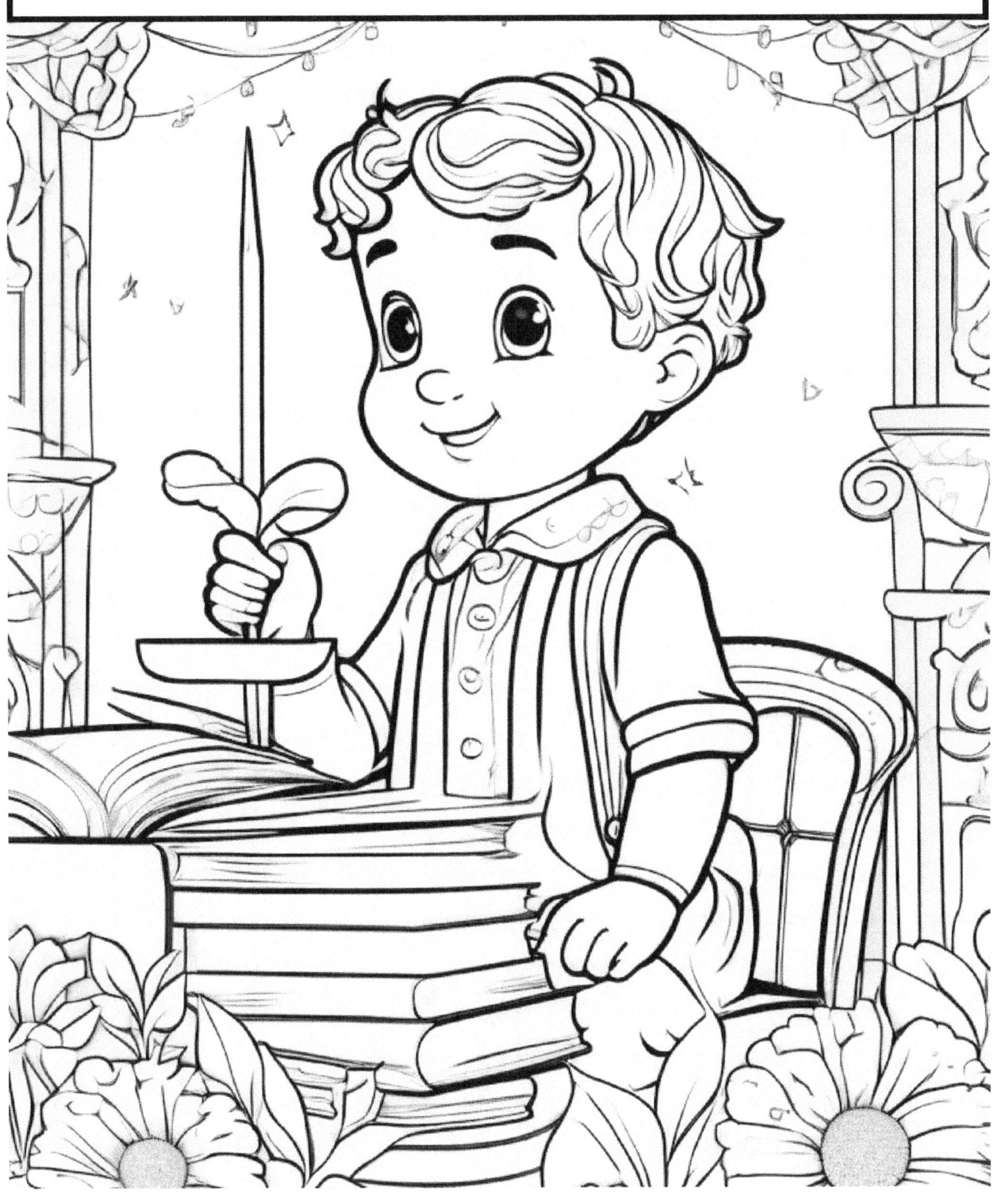

he helped feed the people in the big city.

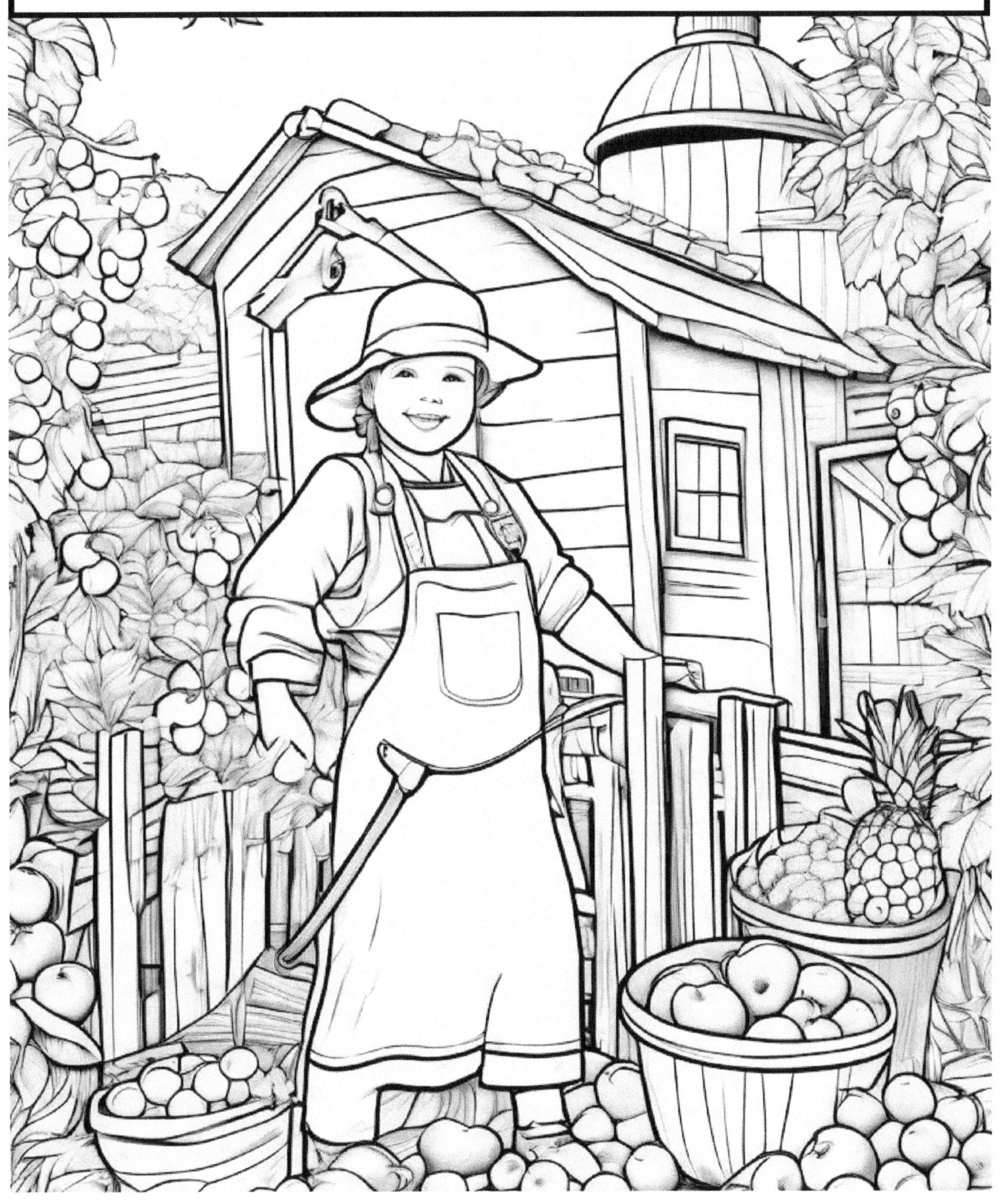

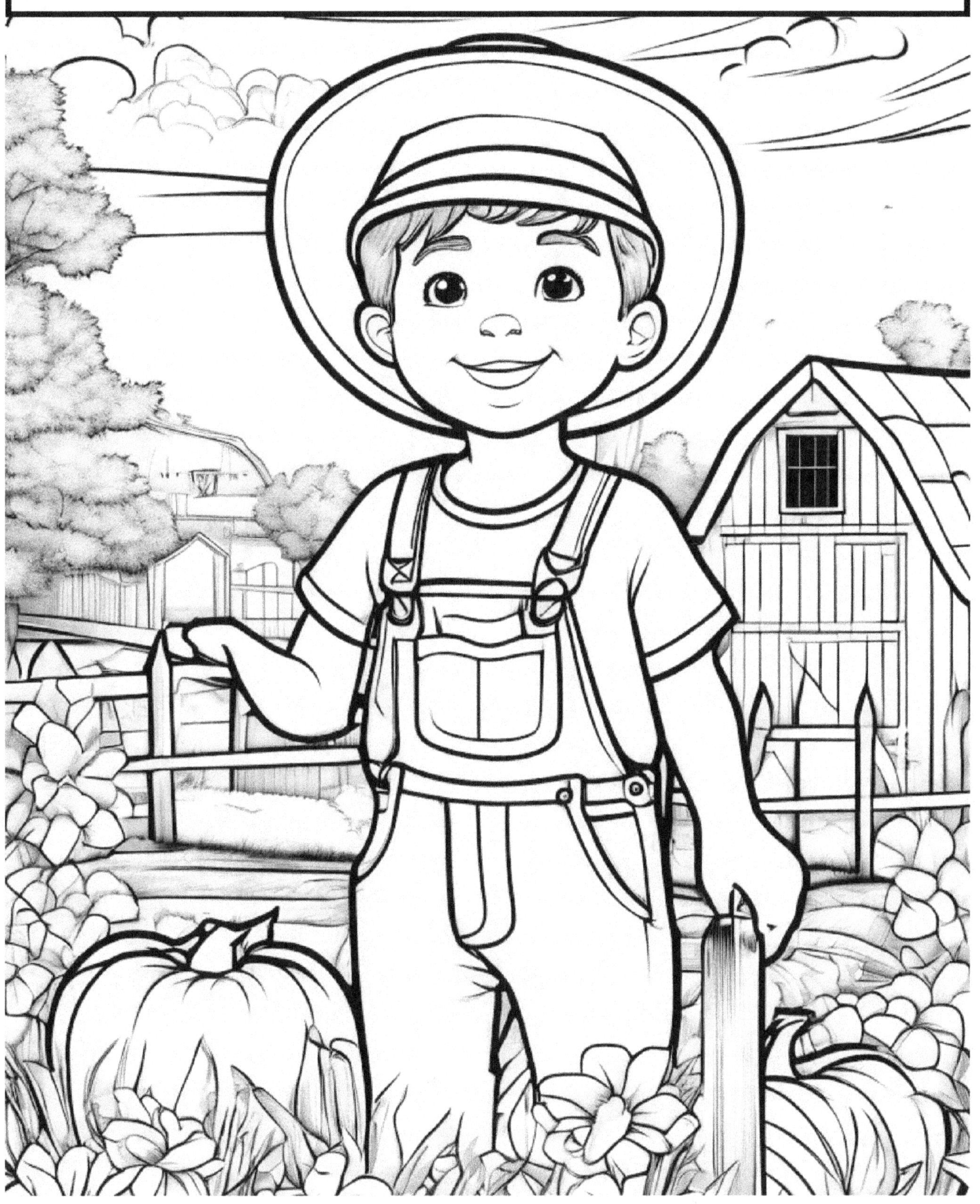

And so Marcus continued to tend his farm.

And everyone who visited his farm left happy.

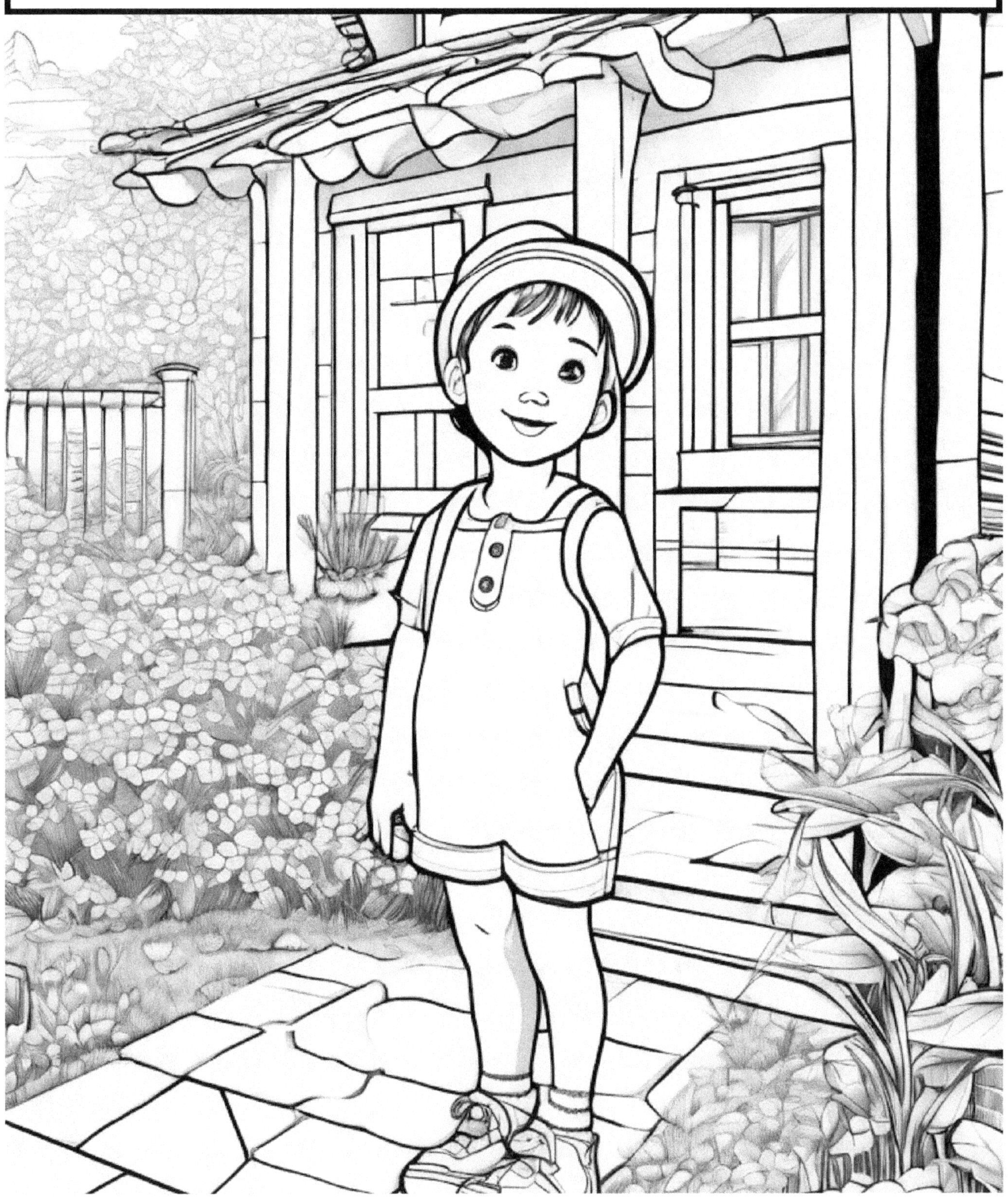

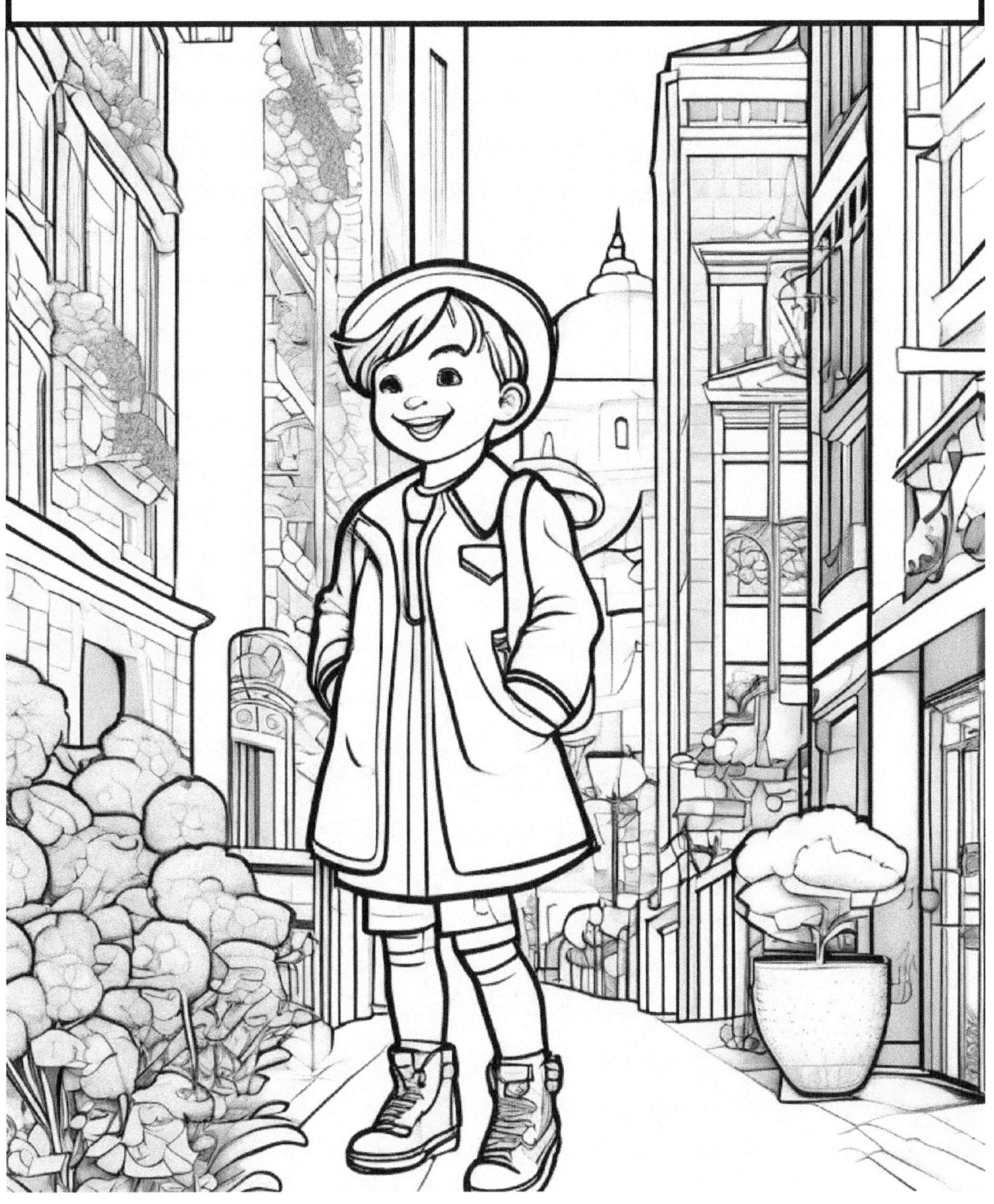

his story spread around the world

Marcus encouraged other farmers in the region.

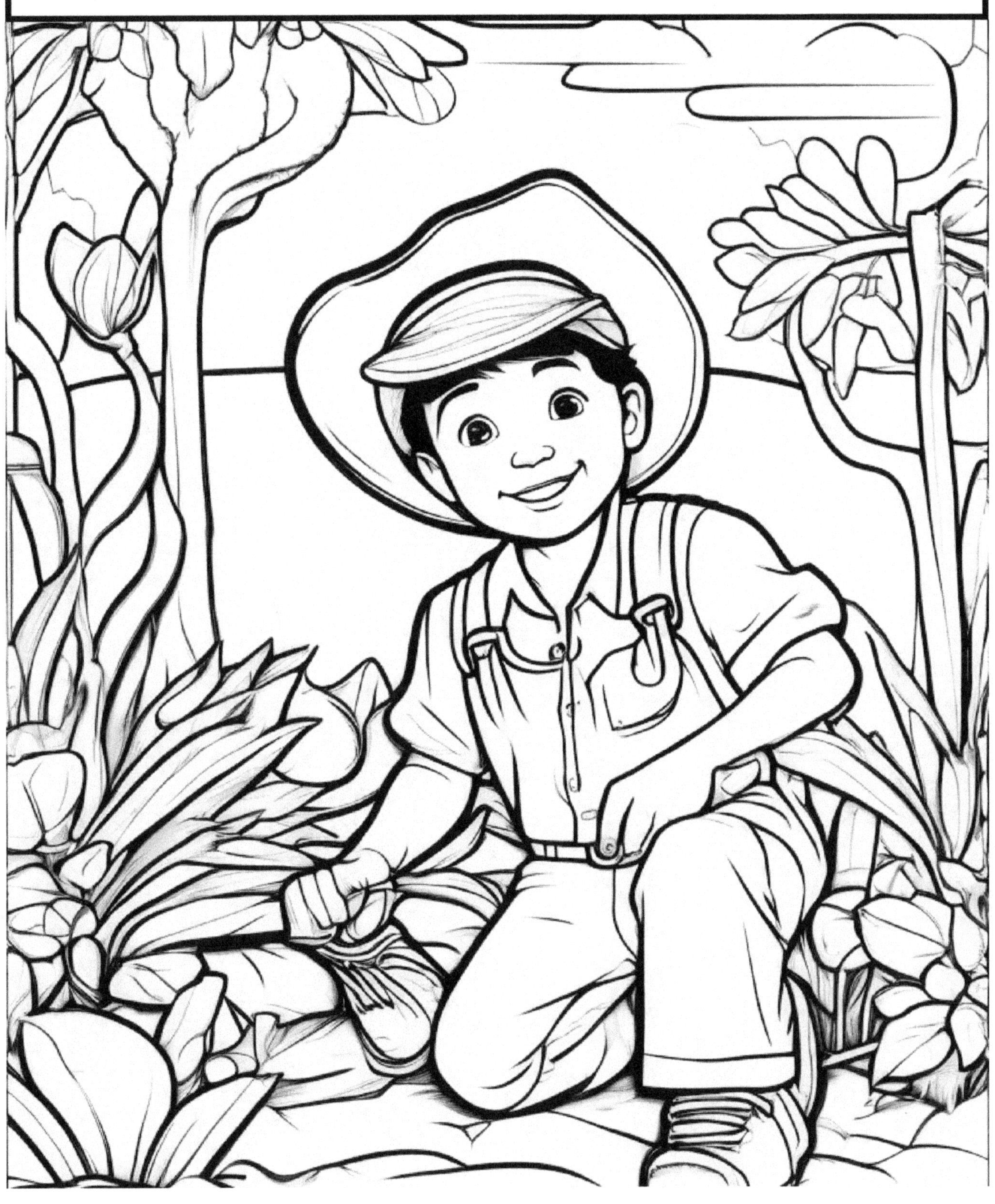

How he cares for and values life in the countryside.

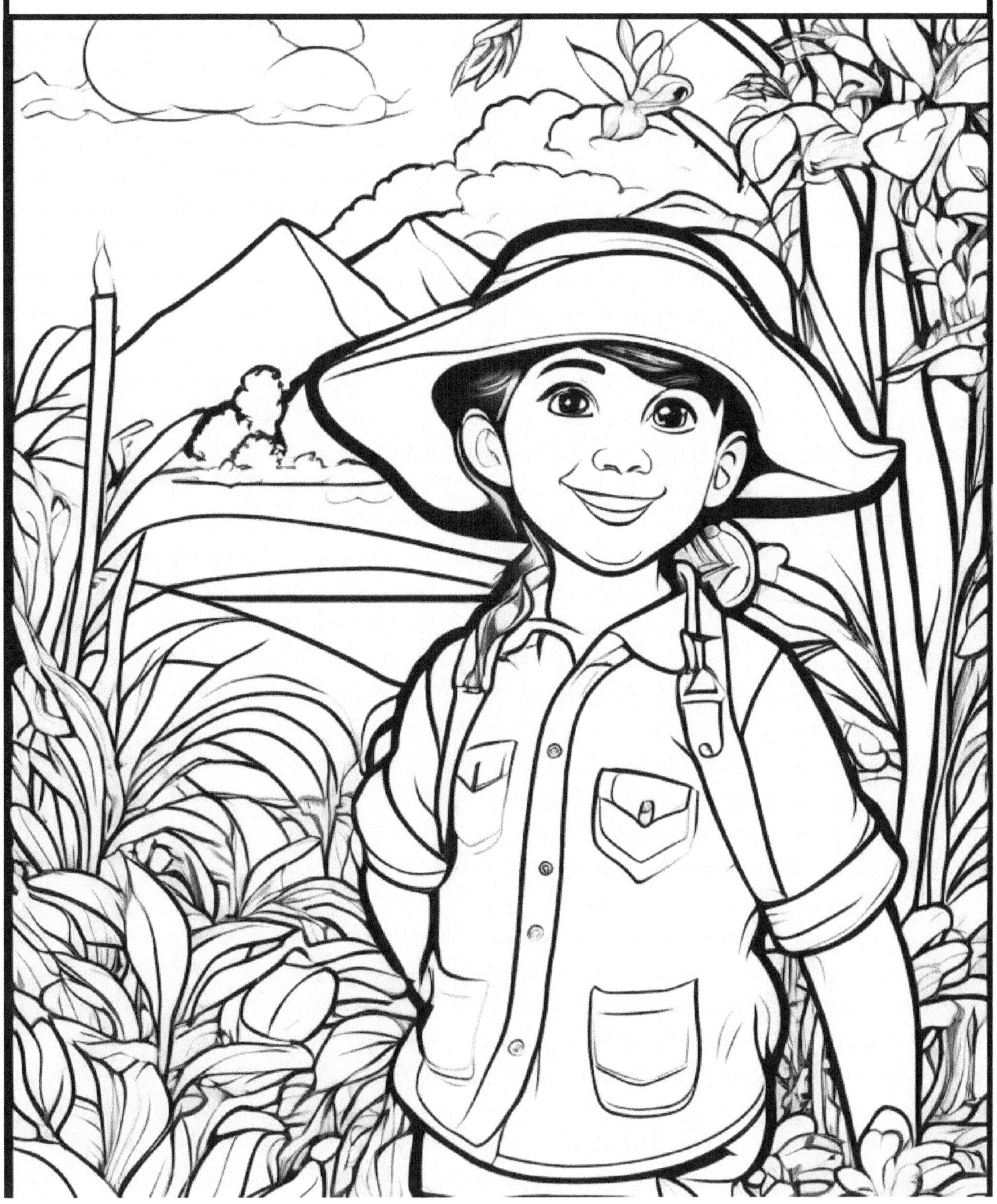

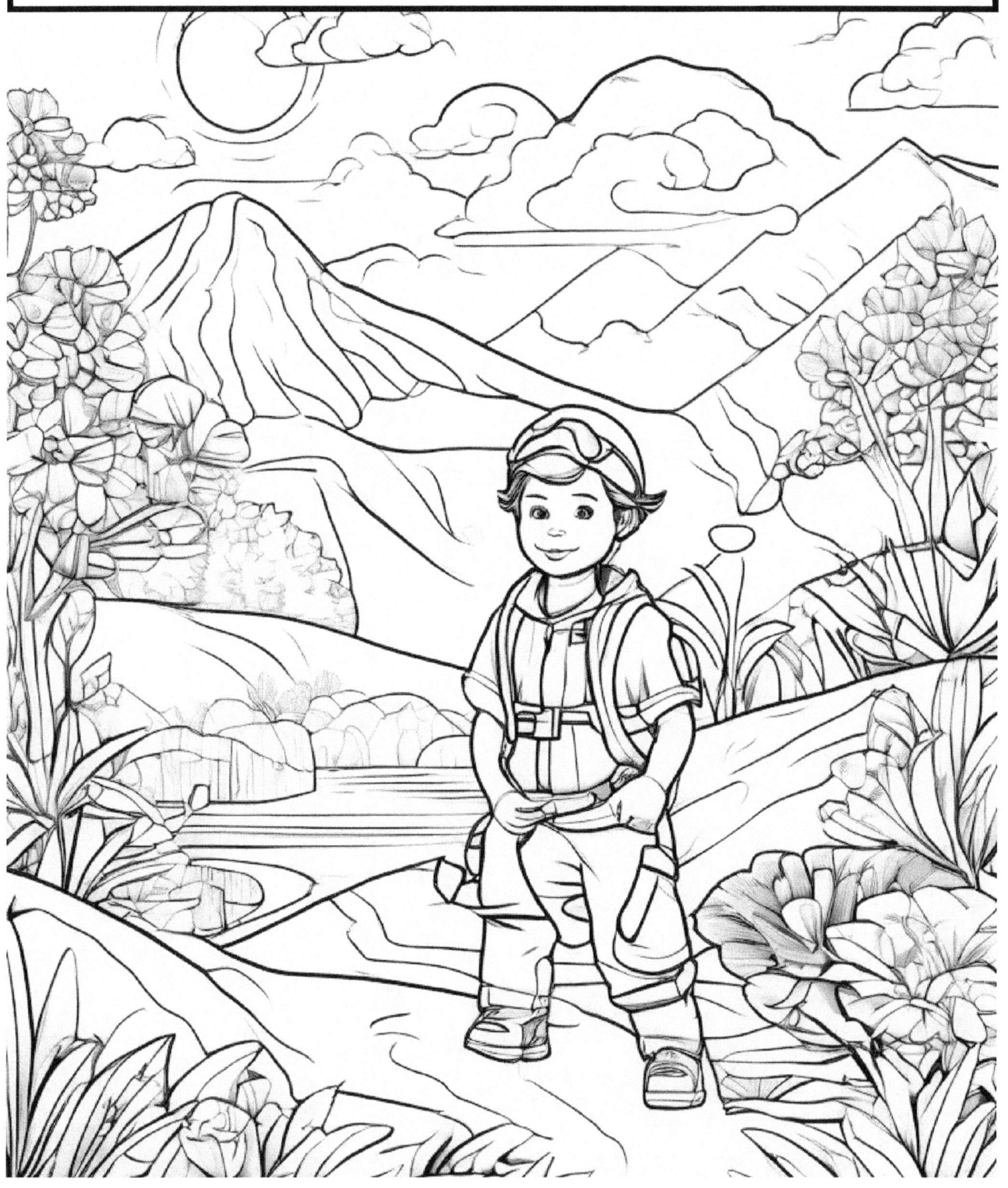

And taking care of the planet we call home.

And so ends this beautiful story of Marcus and his family

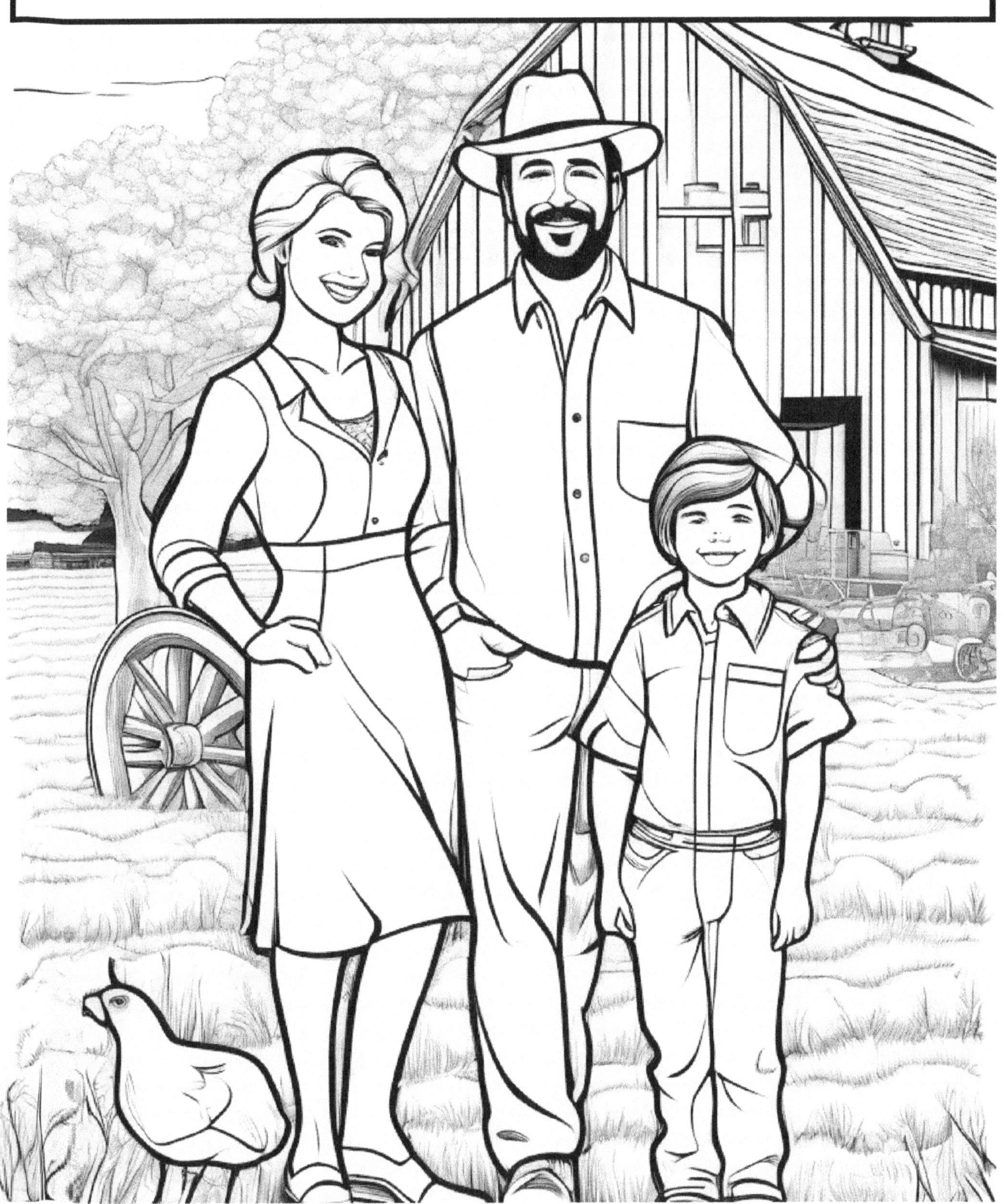